SAT

STANDARD WRITTEN ENGLISH TEST

For College Entrance

by

Gary R. Gruber, Ph.D.

MONARCH PRESS

Published by
MONARCH PRESS
A Simon & Schuster Division of
Gulf & Western Corporation
Simon & Schuster Building
1230 Avenue of the Americas
New York, N.Y. 10020

MONARCH PRESS and colophon are trademarks of Simon & Schuster,
registered in the U.S. Patent and Trademark
Office.

10 9 8 7 6 5 4 3 2 1

Printed in the United States of America

ISBN: 0-671-45884-1

Contents

INTRODUCTION

PART ONE

5 STANDARD WRITTEN ENGLISH PRACTICE TESTS PATTERNED AFTER THE ACTUAL TEST

PART TWO

GRAMMAR AND USAGE REFRESHER

NEW TEST ADDED TO COLLEGE BOARDS

SAT Includes New Half-Hour Examination in Standard Written English

Students who take the Scholastic Aptitute Test for college entrance are now given a new half-hour examination of competence in Standard Written English. This new section measures mastery of English grammar and sentence structure.

The SAT, as before, will continue to be a 3-hour (180-minute) test. But in order to make room for the new Standard Written English test, the Verbal part (previously 90 minutes) has been shortened to 75 minutes and the Math part (previously 90 minutes) has also been shortened to 75 minutes. This allows for the new 30-minute Standard Written English test.

The Verbal and the Math parts of the SAT are graded as before in a range from 200 to 800. The new Standard Written English part is scored separately in a range from 20 to 80.

The new Standard Written English section will be used by most colleges for placement of students in freshman English courses, and not for selection of students for admission. The new section is a response to the concern of many colleges that entering students are unable to write clearly and correctly.

Part One

5 Standard Written English Practice Tests Patterned After the Actual Test

The best way to prepare for the Standard Written English Test is to work with questions that are similar to those which appear on the actual test. In the following pages, you will find five Practice Tests — each very much like the actual Standard Written English test.

These Practice Tests are not copies of the actual test. The actual test is copyrighted and may not be duplicated. The primary purpose of your taking each Practice Test is to help you to diagnose your weaknesses so that you can proceed, without delay, to eliminate those weaknesses.

Each of the five Practice Tests consists of 50 questions with a time limit of 30 minutes — as in the actual Standard Written English test. There are two types of questions in the actual test. Each of the Practice Tests in the following pages includes these two question-types.

Detailed explanatory answers follow each of the five Practice Tests. A very important part of your preparation for the actual test is to study these explanatory answers carefully.

Practice Test 1 ⟶

PRE-TEST TIPS

Should You Guess?

Take "educated guesses." If, in a question, you know that one of the five choices is incorrect, you are at a guessing advantage. One-quarter of a correct answer is deducted for each incorrect answer as a correction for haphazard guessing.

Directions for Each Type of Question in the Test

Familiarize yourself (before you take the test) with the directions for each of the two question-types — (a) Grammar and Usage and (b) Sentence Correction. Not understanding the instructions for a question-type may cause you to lose considerable credit.

USE THIS SHEET FOR YOUR ANSWERS
PRACTICE TEST 1

	A B C D E		A B C D E		A B C D E		A B C D E		A B C D E
1	▯ ▯ ▯ ▯ ▯	11	▯ ▯ ▯ ▯ ▯	21	▯ ▯ ▯ ▯ ▯	31	▯ ▯ ▯ ▯ ▯	41	▯ ▯ ▯ ▯ ▯
2	▯ ▯ ▯ ▯ ▯	12	▯ ▯ ▯ ▯ ▯	22	▯ ▯ ▯ ▯ ▯	32	▯ ▯ ▯ ▯ ▯	42	▯ ▯ ▯ ▯ ▯
3	▯ ▯ ▯ ▯ ▯	13	▯ ▯ ▯ ▯ ▯	23	▯ ▯ ▯ ▯ ▯	33	▯ ▯ ▯ ▯ ▯	43	▯ ▯ ▯ ▯ ▯
4	▯ ▯ ▯ ▯ ▯	14	▯ ▯ ▯ ▯ ▯	24	▯ ▯ ▯ ▯ ▯	34	▯ ▯ ▯ ▯ ▯	44	▯ ▯ ▯ ▯ ▯
5	▯ ▯ ▯ ▯ ▯	15	▯ ▯ ▯ ▯ ▯	25	▯ ▯ ▯ ▯ ▯	35	▯ ▯ ▯ ▯ ▯	45	▯ ▯ ▯ ▯ ▯
6	▯ ▯ ▯ ▯ ▯	16	▯ ▯ ▯ ▯ ▯	26	▯ ▯ ▯ ▯ ▯	36	▯ ▯ ▯ ▯ ▯	46	▯ ▯ ▯ ▯ ▯
7	▯ ▯ ▯ ▯ ▯	17	▯ ▯ ▯ ▯ ▯	27	▯ ▯ ▯ ▯ ▯	37	▯ ▯ ▯ ▯ ▯	47	▯ ▯ ▯ ▯ ▯
8	▯ ▯ ▯ ▯ ▯	18	▯ ▯ ▯ ▯ ▯	28	▯ ▯ ▯ ▯ ▯	38	▯ ▯ ▯ ▯ ▯	48	▯ ▯ ▯ ▯ ▯
9	▯ ▯ ▯ ▯ ▯	19	▯ ▯ ▯ ▯ ▯	29	▯ ▯ ▯ ▯ ▯	39	▯ ▯ ▯ ▯ ▯	49	▯ ▯ ▯ ▯ ▯
10	▯ ▯ ▯ ▯ ▯	20	▯ ▯ ▯ ▯ ▯	30	▯ ▯ ▯ ▯ ▯	40	▯ ▯ ▯ ▯ ▯	50	▯ ▯ ▯ ▯ ▯

Note: At the actual test you will be given an Answer Sheet very much like this sheet in order to record your answers. In doing the following Practice Test, you may prefer to use this Practice Test Answer Sheet. It may, however, be more convenient for you to mark your answer right next to each question. For this method of recording answers, an answer space is, as you will see, provided with each question in this Practice Test.

Standard Written English Practice Test 1

Time: 30 Minutes for the Entire Test

SECTION ONE: GRAMMAR AND USAGE

Directions: In each question, you will find a sentence with four words (or phrases) underlined. In some sentences one of the underlined words (or phrases) is incorrect in the light of the rules of standard written English for grammar, correct usage, and choice of words. No sentence has more than one error. You are to assume that the rest of the sentence (whatever is not underlined) is correct. If you find an error, choose the letter (A *or* B *or* C *or* D) of that underlined word (or phrase) which is incorrect. If you find no error, fill in answer space E.

1. The <u>union</u> delegates who <u>are going</u> to the convention <u>in Miami Beach</u>
   A · · · · · · · · · · · · · · · B · · · · · · · · · · · · · · · C

   are Thompson, Steinmetz, and <u>me</u>. <u>No error</u>.
   · · · · · · · · · · · · · · · · · · · D · · · · E

          A B C D E
   1 ☐ ☐ ☐ ☐ ☐

2. After being wheeled <u>into</u> the <u>infirmary</u>, the <u>nurse</u> at the desk asked
   · · · · · · · · · · · · · · · A · · · · · · · · B · · · · · · · · C

   me <u>several</u> questions. <u>No error</u>.
   · · · · D · · · · · · · · · · · · · E

          A B C D E
   2 ☐ ☐ ☐ ☐ ☐

3. <u>Us</u> boys insist on <u>your</u> giving them what is <u>theirs</u> and us what is
   A · · · · · · · · · · · · · · B · · · · · · · · · · · · · · C

   <u>ours</u>. <u>No error</u>.
   D · · · E

          A B C D E
   3 ☐ ☐ ☐ ☐ ☐

4. We hear <u>dissent</u> from a young man who, we <u>firmly</u> believe, is not
   · · · · · · · A · B

   about <u>to pay</u> compliments to our political leaders <u>or</u> to the local
   · · · · · · · C · D

   draft board. <u>No error</u>.
   · · · · · · · · · · · E

          A B C D E
   4 ☐ ☐ ☐ ☐ ☐

5. She <u>wore a dress</u> to the party that was far <u>more</u> attractive than
   · · · · A · · · · · · · · · · B · · · · · · · · · · · · C

   <u>the other</u> girls. <u>No error</u>.
   · · · D · · · · · · · · · E

          A B C D E
   5 ☐ ☐ ☐ ☐ ☐

6. Controversial matters <u>involving</u> the two groups <u>were discussed</u>; never-
   · · · · · · · · · · · · · · · · · A · · · · · · · · · · · · · B

   theless, <u>most</u> of the representatives <u>remained calm</u>. <u>No error</u>.
   · · · · · · · C · · · · · · · · · · · · · · · · D · · · · · · · · E

          A B C D E
   6 ☐ ☐ ☐ ☐ ☐

7

7. If he had laid quietly under the tree as he had been instructed to do,
   $\overline{}$ $\overline{}$ $\overline{}$
   A   B   C

   we would have found him. No error.
   $\overline{}$ $\overline{}$
   D   E

7 A B C D E
   ☐ ☐ ☐ ☐ ☐

8. If one reads a great many articles in *Elementary English,* you will
   $\overline{}$ $\overline{}$
   A   B

   become familiar with the problems of the beginning teacher of read-
   $\overline{}$ $\overline{}$
   C   D

   ing. No error.
   $\overline{}$
   E

8 A B C D E
   ☐ ☐ ☐ ☐ ☐

9. Down the field came the students of South High School: members of
   $\overline{}$
   A

   the newly organized, somewhat incompetent band; drum majorettes
   $\overline{}$
   B

   in white, spangled skirts; and the team, muddy and wretched.
   $\overline{}$ $\overline{}$
   C   D

   No error.
   $\overline{}$
   E

9 A B C D E
   ☐ ☐ ☐ ☐ ☐

10. If I would have been there, I certainly would have taken care of the
    $\overline{}$ $\overline{}$ $\overline{}$
    A   B   C

    problem in a hurry. No error.
    $\overline{}$ $\overline{}$
    D   E

10 A B C D E
    ☐ ☐ ☐ ☐ ☐

11. Between you and I, I am convinced that this painting by Dali shows
    $\overline{}$ $\overline{}$
    A   B

    greater artistry than that of Picasso. No error.
    $\overline{}$ $\overline{}$ $\overline{}$
    C   D   E

11 A B C D E
    ☐ ☐ ☐ ☐ ☐

12. He believes in witchcraft, but he doubts that they ride on broom-
    $\overline{}$ $\overline{}$ $\overline{}$ $\overline{}$
    A   B   C   D

    sticks. No error.
    $\overline{}$
    E

12 A B C D E
    ☐ ☐ ☐ ☐ ☐

13. Being that you are interested in the outcome of the election, let us
    $\overline{}$ $\overline{}$ $\overline{}$
    A   B   C

    wait until the final tally has been made. No error.
    $\overline{}$ $\overline{}$
    D   E

13 A B C D E
    ☐ ☐ ☐ ☐ ☐

14. The retreat of the enemy soldiers into caves and tunnels are deceiving
    $\overline{}$ $\overline{}$
    A   B

    the oncoming infantrymen. No error.
    $\overline{}$ $\overline{}$ $\overline{}$
    C   D   E

14 A B C D E
    ☐ ☐ ☐ ☐ ☐

15. The millennium will have arrived when parents give appropriate
       $\overline{\text{A}}$ $\overline{\text{B}}$ $\overline{\text{C}}$

responsibilities to we teenagers. No error.
                    $\overline{\text{D}}$ $\overline{\text{E}}$

15 A B C D E ☐ ☐ ☐ ☐ ☐

16. In contrast to Arnold's intellectual prowess was his slovenly appear-
      $\overline{\text{A}}$ $\overline{\text{B}}$ $\overline{\text{C}}$ $\overline{\text{D}}$

ance and his nervous demeanor. No error.
                                $\overline{\text{E}}$

16 A B C D E ☐ ☐ ☐ ☐ ☐

17. The crisis in the Middle East is one of the topics that
             $\overline{\text{A}}$ $\overline{\text{B}}$

has been discussed at our weekly forums. No error.
$\overline{\text{C}}$ $\overline{\text{D}}$ $\overline{\text{E}}$

17 A B C D E ☐ ☐ ☐ ☐ ☐

18. I wouldn't be interested in buying this here farm even if you were
     $\overline{\text{A}}$ $\overline{\text{B}}$ $\overline{\text{C}}$ $\overline{\text{D}}$

to offer it to me for a hundred dollars. No error.
                                    $\overline{\text{E}}$

18 A B C D E ☐ ☐ ☐ ☐ ☐

19. The trouble with a good many people in our country is that they
              $\overline{\text{A}}$

have vested interests — that is, they are concerned with theirselves
     $\overline{\text{B}}$ $\overline{\text{C}}$ $\overline{\text{D}}$
first and foremost. No error.
                $\overline{\text{E}}$

19 A B C D E ☐ ☐ ☐ ☐ ☐

20. There is no sense in getting angry with them radicals just because
                       $\overline{\text{A}}$ $\overline{\text{B}}$ $\overline{\text{C}}$

they disagree with you. No error.
              $\overline{\text{D}}$ $\overline{\text{E}}$

20 A B C D E ☐ ☐ ☐ ☐ ☐

21. There seem nowadays to be little of the optimism that imbued our
           $\overline{\text{A}}$ $\overline{\text{B}}$ $\overline{\text{C}}$

ancestors with courage and hope. No error.
            $\overline{\text{D}}$ $\overline{\text{E}}$

21 A B C D E ☐ ☐ ☐ ☐ ☐

22. The high school graduate, if he is eighteen or nineteen, has these
                                  $\overline{\text{A}}$ $\overline{\text{B}}$

alternatives: attending college, finding a job, or the army. No error.
$\overline{\text{C}}$ $\overline{\text{D}}$ $\overline{\text{E}}$

22 A B C D E ☐ ☐ ☐ ☐ ☐

23. Since it was an <u>unusually</u> warm day, the dog <u>laid</u> under the tree
    A   B

<u>all afternoon</u> without barking at <u>passersby</u> — something he
    C   D

usually does. <u>No error.</u>
              E

23 A B C D E
   □ □ □ □ □

24. There <u>was</u> only an apple and three pears <u>in the refrigerator</u> when
          A   B

we <u>came home</u> after a <u>weekend</u> in the country. <u>No error.</u>
    C   D   E

24 A B C D E
   □ □ □ □ □

25. The Chairman <u>of the Board</u> of Directors made it <u>clear</u> at the meeting
                 A   B

that he <u>will not</u> step down from his position <u>as chairman.</u> <u>No error.</u>
        C   D   E

25 A B C D E
   □ □ □ □ □

26. Although Hank was the captain of our high school track team, and

<u>was hailed</u> as the fastest man on the team, I have <u>no doubt about</u>
    A   B

<u>my being able</u> to run faster than <u>him</u> today. <u>No error.</u>
    C   D   E

26 A B C D E
   □ □ □ □ □

27. <u>These kind</u> of people who have little education, who have no desire
    A

for cultural pursuits, and whose sole purpose <u>is acquiring</u> wealth,
                                               B

are not the <u>type</u> I wish <u>to associate with.</u> <u>No error.</u>
            C   D   E

27 A B C D E
   □ □ □ □ □

28. <u>Whether</u> the sales campaign <u>succeeds</u> <u>will probably not be known</u> for
    A   B   C

at least a year, but it is clear now that the stakes <u>are high.</u> <u>No error.</u>
                                                      D   E

28 A B C D E
   □ □ □ □ □

29. Neither Sam Atkins <u>nor</u> Henry Miller, sales representatives for the
                       A

company, presented <u>their</u> summaries of sales <u>before</u> the deadline
                   B   C

<u>for doing so.</u> <u>No error.</u>
    D   E

29 A B C D E
   □ □ □ □ □

30. A recent poll <u>has indicated</u> that Harold, who is a senior at South Palmetto
A

High School, is considered <u>brighter</u> <u>than any</u> student <u>in the senior class</u>
B   C   D

at that school. <u>No error.</u>
E

               A B C D E

30 ⬚ ⬚ ⬚ ⬚ ⬚

SECTION TWO: SENTENCE CORRECTION

Directions: Each sentence is partly or wholly underlined. In some cases, what is underlined is correct — in other cases, it is incorrect. The five choices that follow each sentence represent various ways of writing the underlined part. Choice A is the same as the original underlining but Choices B, C, D, and E are different. If, in your judgment, the original sentence is better than any of the changed sentences, select Choice A. If another choice produces the only correct sentence, select that other choice (B or C or D or E).

In making your choice, you should observe the rules of standard written English. Your choice must fulfill the requirements of correct grammar, diction (word choice), sentence structure, and punctuation.

If a choice changes the meaning of the original sentence, do not make that choice.

31. Driving a racing car on a speedway <u>is in some ways like when you are riding</u> a horse on a bridle path.

    (A) is in some ways like when you are riding
    (B) in some ways is in the same class as riding
    (C) is in some ways similar to when you are riding
    (D) is in some ways similar to riding
    (E) is like a ride in some ways of

                                                   A B C D E
                                              31 ⦾ ⦾ ⦾ ⦾ ⦾

32. <u>Seeing their father, the cigarettes were immediately concealed by the children.</u>

    (A) Seeing their father, the cigarettes were immediately concealed by the children.
    (B) Their father being seen by them, the children immediately concealed the cigarettes.
    (C) The children having seen their father, the cigarettes were concealed immediately.
    (D) When the children saw their father, they immediately concealed the cigarettes.
    (E) When their father was seen, the children immediately concealed the cigarettes.

                                                   A B C D E
                                             32 ⦾ ⦾ ⦾ ⦾ ⦾

33. <u>Barrymore had many wives, Garrick one,</u> but each is remembered not for his women but for his talent.

    (A) Barrymore had many wives, Garrick one
    (B) Barrymore had many wives, Garrick having one
    (C) Barrymore having many wives, Garrick just one
    (D) Barrymore has had many wives, but Garrick only one
    (E) Barrymore had many wives, Garrick had only one wife

                                                   A B C D E
                                             33 ⦾ ⦾ ⦾ ⦾ ⦾

34. Biologists often say that <u>it is not chemists or physicists but that they have</u> the answer to the improvement of life on earth.

    (A) it is not chemists or physicists but that they have
    (B) it is not chemists or physicists but they have
    (C) they, and not chemists or physicists have
    (D) it is not chemists or physicists but it is they who have
    (E) it is they, not chemists or physicists, who have

    34 A B C D E 🔲🔲🔲🔲🔲

35. The underprivileged student is getting a better <u>education, there are better teachers for them</u> and better facilities.

    (A) education, there are better teachers for them
    (B) education; he has better teachers
    (C) education; they have better teachers
    (D) education, he has better teachers
    (E) education; because he has better teachers

    35 A B C D E 🔲🔲🔲🔲🔲

36. <u>When the university administration changed its role from that of a judge and prosecutor to that of an adviser and friend,</u> not only did the students stop their demonstrations but they also sided with the administration against the outsiders.

    (A) When the university administration changed its role from that of a judge and prosecutor to that of an adviser and friend
    (B) When the university administration changed its role from that of a judge and prosecutor to an adviser and friend
    (C) When the university administration changed its role from that of a judge and prosecutor to one of an adviser and friend
    (D) As a result of the administration's changing its role from judge and prosecutor to that of adviser and friend
    (E) As to the university administration, in changing its role from that of a judge and prosecutor to that of an adviser and friend

    36 A B C D E 🔲🔲🔲🔲🔲

37. The Soviet Union has reorganized and modernized its intelligence network in the Western Hemisphere toward the goal of diminishing and <u>to possibly replace</u> United States influence.

    (A) to possibly replace
    (B) possibly to replace
    (C) possibly replacing
    (D) to replace possibly
    (E) for replacement of

    37 A B C D E 🔲🔲🔲🔲🔲

38. In the next booklet, <u>the sales manager and personnel director will tell</u> <u>you something about his work.</u>

 (A) the sales manager and personnel director will tell you something about his work

 (B) the sales manager who is also director of personnel will tell you something about their work

 (C) the sales manager who is also personnel director will tell you something

 (D) the sales manager and personnel director will tell you something as it applies to his work

 (E) the sales manager and the personnel director will tell you something about what his work is

                   A B C D E
                   38 0 0 0 0 0

39. I have enjoyed the study of the Spanish language not only because of its beauty but also <u>to make use of it in business.</u>

 (A) to make use of it in business

 (B) because of its use in business

 (C) on account it is useful in business

 (D) one needs it in business

 (E) since all business people use it

                   A B C D E
                   39 0 0 0 0 0

40. Known to every man, woman, and child in the town, <u>friends were</u> <u>never lacking to my grandfather.</u>

 (A) friends were never lacking to my grandfather

 (B) my grandfather was not lacking to his friends

 (C) friends never lacked my grandfather

 (D) my grandfather never lacked no friends

 (E) my grandfather never lacked friends

                   A B C D E
                   40 0 0 0 0 0

41. No sooner had he entered the room <u>when the lights went out</u> and everybody began to scream.

 (A) when the lights went out

 (B) than the lights went out

 (C) and the lights went out

 (D) but the lights went out

 (E) the lights went out

                   A B C D E
                   41 0 0 0 0 0

42. John, whose mother is a teacher, <u>is not so good a student as many</u> <u>other friends</u> I have with no academic background in their families.

 (A) is not so good a student as many other friends

 (B) is not as good a student like many other friends

 (C) is not quite the student as are other friends

 (D) as a student is not a good as many other friends

 (E) does not have the studious qualities of many other friends

                   A B C D E
                   42 0 0 0 0 0

43. After our waiting in line for three hours, <u>much to our disgust, the tickets had been sold out</u> when we reached the window.

    (A) much to our disgust, the tickets had been sold out
    (B) the tickets had been, much to our disgust, sold out
    (C) the tickets had been sold out, much to our disgust,
    (D) the sold-out tickets had, much to our disgust, been disposed of
    (E) and much to our disgust, the tickets had been sold out

43   A B C D E   ⬚ ⬚ ⬚ ⬚ ⬚

44. When the members of the committee are at odds, <u>and when also, in addition, they are in the process</u> of offering their resignations, problems become indissoluble.

    (A) and when also, in addition, they are in the process
    (B) and also when they are in the process
    (C) and when, in addition, they are in the process
    (D) they are in the process
    (E) and when the members of the committee are in the process

44   A B C D E   ⬚ ⬚ ⬚ ⬚ ⬚

45. <u>There is no objection to him joining the party</u> if he is willing to fit in with the plans of the group.

    (A) There is no objection to him joining the party
    (B) There is no objection on him joining the party
    (C) There is no objection to his joining the party
    (D) No objection will be raised upon him joining the party
    (E) If he decides to join the party, there will be no objection

45   A B C D E   ⬚ ⬚ ⬚ ⬚ ⬚

46. Further acquaintance with the memoirs of Elizabeth Barrett Browning and Robert Browning enables us to appreciate the depth of influence that two people <u>of talent can have on one another.</u>

    (A) of talent can have on one another
    (B) of talent can exert on one another
    (C) with talent can have one for the other
    (D) of talent can have on each other
    (E) who are talented can have

46   A B C D E   ⬚ ⬚ ⬚ ⬚ ⬚

47. <u>If you saw the amount of pancakes he consumed</u> at breakfast this morning, you would understand why he is so overweight.

    (A) If you saw the amount of pancakes he consumed
    (B) If you would see the amount of pancakes he consumed
    (C) When you see the amount of pancakes he consumed
    (D) If you saw the number of pancakes he consumed
    (E) If you had seen the number of pancakes he consumed

47   A B C D E   ⬚ ⬚ ⬚ ⬚ ⬚

48. The debutante went to the concert with her fiancé wearing a sheer blouse.

   (A) The debutante went to the concert with her fiancé wearing a sheer blouse.
   (B) The debutante went to the concert, wearing a sheer blouse, with her fiancé.
   (C) The debutante, wearing a sheer blouse, went to the concert with her fiancé.
   (D) With her fiancé, wearing a sheer blouse, the debutante went to the concert.
   (E) To the concert, wearing a sheer blouse, went the debutante with her fiancé.

   48 A B C D E

49. Briefly the functions of a military staff are to advise the commander, transmit his instructions, and the supervision of the execution of his decisions.

   (A) and the supervision of the execution of his decisions
   (B) also the supervision of the execution of his decisions
   (C) and supervising the execution of his decisions
   (D) and supervise the execution of his decisions
   (E) and have supervision of the execution of his decisions

   49 A B C D E

50. The 15-round decision that Frazier was given over Ali was not popular with all of the boxing fans.

   (A) The 15-round decision that Frazier was given over Ali
   (B) Frazier's 15-round decision over Ali
   (C) The Frazier 15-round decision over Ali
   (D) The decision of 15 rounds that Frazier was given over Ali
   (E) Ali's 15-round decision that Frazier was given over him

   50 A B C D E

NOW THAT YOU HAVE COMPLETED PRACTICE TEST 1

1. Turn to the Answer Key on page 18.
2. How many **correct answers** do you have out of 50 questions? ....
3. How many **incorrect answers** do you have out of 50 questions? ....
4. Deduct ¼ of the number of incorrect answers from the number of correct answers to get a **"raw score"** of ....
5. Your **"scaled score"** for this test, according to the Raw Score/Scaled Score Table on page 24 is ....

ANSWER KEY FOR PRACTICE TEST 1

1. D	11. A	21. A	31. D	41. B
2. C	12. C	22. D	32. D	42. A
3. A	13. A	23. B	33. A	43. C
4. E	14. B	24. A	34. E	44. C
5. D	15. D	25. C	35. B	45. C
6. E	16. C	26. D	36. A	46. D
7. A	17. E	27. A	37. C	47. E
8. B	18. B	28. E	38. A	48. C
9. E	19. D	29. B	39. B	49. D
10. B	20. B	30. C	40. E	50. A

EXPLANATORY ANSWERS
FOR PRACTICE TEST 1

1. **(D)** ". . . are Thompson, Steinmetz, and *I*."
The predicate nominative form is *I* (not *me*).

2. **(C)** ". . . into the infirmary, *I* was asked several questions by the nurse at the desk."
It is *I* who was being wheeled—not the *nurse*. The participial construction should modify the subject. In the original sentence, the subject is *nurse*.

3. **(A)** "*We* boys insist . . ."
The pronoun-adjective which modifies a subject (*boys* in this case) must take the subject form *we* (not *us*).

4. **(E)** All underlined parts are correct.

5. **(D)** ". . . than *those* of the other girls."
We have an improper ellipsis here. The dress that the girl wore was more attractive than the dresses of the other girls—not more attractive than the other girls.

6. **(E)** All underlined parts are correct.

7. **(A)** "If he *had lain* . . ."
The past perfect tense form of *to lie* is *had lain* (not *had laid*). The past perfect tense form of *to lay*—meaning to place or to put—is *had laid*.

8. **(B)** ". . . *one* will become . . ."
Do not shift the number or person of a noun if the noun represents another noun which precedes in the sentence. In the original sentence, *one* and *you* refer to the same person. Since *one* is third person and *you* is second person, we have a shift error.

9. **(E)** All underlined parts are correct.

10. **(B)** "If I *had been* there . . ."
In a contrary-to-fact conditional construction in past time, sequence of tenses requires the past perfect subjunctive form (*had been*) in the "if" clause instead of the future perfect subjunctive form (*would have been*).

11. **(A)** "Between you and *me* . . ."
The object of the preposition *between* must be an objective case form (*me*—not *I*).

12. **(C)** ". . . that *witches* ride on broomsticks."
The pronoun *they* must have an antecedent, which is obviously *witchcraft*. But since witchcraft is a singular abstract noun, the plural personal pronoun *they* cannot be used here. Accordingly, we must substitute a noun, such as *witches,* for the pronoun. The word *witches,* of course, has no antecedent because it is a noun. Only pronouns have antecedents.

13. **(A)** "*Since* you are interested . . ."
Being that is unacceptable for *since* or *because*.

14. **(B)** ". . . into caves and tunnels *is deceiving* . . ."
Since the subject (*retreat*) is singular, the verb must be singular (*is* deceiving—not *are* deceiving).

15. **(D)** ". . . to *us* teenagers."
The pronoun-adjective modifying the object of the preposition must be objective in form. *Teenagers* is the object of the preposition *to*. The pronoun-adjective modifying teenagers must, therefore, be the object form (*us*—not *we*).

16. **(C)** ". . . *were* his slovenly appearance and his nervous demeanor."
The two subjects (*appearance* and *demeanor*) constitute plurality. We must, accordingly, have a plural verb (*were*—not *was*).

17. **(E)** All underlined parts are correct.

18. **(B)** ". . . in buying *this farm* . . ."
The expression *this here* is unacceptable for *this*.

19. **(D)** ". . . are concerned with *themselves* . . ."
The correct form of the reflexive pronoun is *themselves*—not *theirselves*.

20. **(B)** ". . . angry with *those* radicals . . ."
The adjective-pronoun *those* must be used to modify the noun *radicals*. The pronoun *them* cannot be used to modify a noun.

21. **(A)** "There *seems* nowadays little of the optimism . . ."
The subject of the sentence (*little*) is singular and it therefore takes a singular verb (*seems* – not *seem*).

22. **(D)** ". . . attending college, finding a job, or *joining the army*."
The need for parallelism requires *joining the army,* in order to have a balanced construction with the preceding gerund phrases (*attending college* and *finding a job*).

23. **(B)** ". . . the dog *lay* under the tree . . ."
The past tense of the verb *lie* is *lay* — not *laid*.

24. **(A)** "There *were* only an apple an three pears . . ." The subject of the sentence is plural (*an apple and three pears*). Therefore the verb must be plural (*were* — not *was*). Incidentally, the word *there* is not the subject — it is an expletive.

25. **(C)** ". . . that he *would* not step down . . ." Since the verb of the main clause (*made*) is in the past tense, the verb of the subordinate clause must also be in the past tense (*would speak*). Incidentally, *would speak* is a past subjunctive.

26. **(D)** ". . . no doubt about my being able to run faster than *he* today." The nominative case (*he* — not *him*) must be used after the conjunction *than* when the pronoun is the subject of an elliptical clause ("than he can run today").

27. **(A)** "*These kinds* of people . . ."
A plural pronoun-adjective (*These* — not *this*) must be used to modify a plural noun (*kinds*).

28. **(E)** All underlined parts are correct.

29. **(B)** ". . . presented *his* summaries of sales . . .
Singular antecedents (*Atkins* and *Miller*) which are joined by *or* or *nor* are referred to by singular pronouns (*his*, in this case — not *their*).

30. **(C)** ". . . brighter than *any other* student . . .
As the original sentence stands, Harold is brighter than himself. In a comparative construction, we must be sure that, if A and B are compared, A is not included as part of B.

31. **(D)** Choice A is incorrect because "like when" is ungrammatical. Choice B is incorrect because it is too indirect. Choice C is incorrect because "similar to when" is ungrammatical. Choice D is correct. Choice E is incorrect because it is awkwardly expressed.

32. **(D)** Choice A is incorrect because the present participle "Seeing" is incorrectly modifying "the cigarettes." Choices B, C, and E are too roundabout. Choice D is correct.

33. **(A)** Choice A is correct. Choice B is incorrect because the nominative absolute construction "Garrick having one" throws the sentence out of balance. Choice C is incorrect because we need a finite verb ("had"), not the participle "having". Choice D is incorrect because the present perfect tense ("has had") should be replaced by the past tense ("had"). Choice E is too wordy.

34. **(E)** Choice A is incorrect because it is awkward and because the pronoun "they" has an indefinite antecedent. Choice B is incorrect for the same reason. Choice C is incorrect — it would be correct if changed to "they, not chemists and physicists, have." Choice D is too wordy. Choice E is correct.

35. **(B)** Choice A is incorrect because we have a run-on sentence. The comma should be replaced by a semicolon or a period. Choice A is incorrect for another reason: the singular pronoun "him" (not "them") should be used because the antecedent ("student") of the pronoun is singular. Choice B is correct. Choice C is incorrect because the pronoun "they" should be singular. Choice D is incorrect because it creates a run-on sentence. Choice E is incorrect — the semicolon should be eliminated.

36. **(A)** Choice A is correct. Choice B is incorrect because of the improper ellipsis of the words "that of" which should precede "an adviser and friend." Choice C is incorrect, because the word "one" should be replaced by the words "that of." Choices D and E are incorrect because they are too indirect. Moreover, in Choice D, right after the words "its role" we should place the words "that of."

37. **(C)** Choice A is incorrect because we should have a gerund ("replacing") to balance with the previous gerund ("diminishing." Moreover, there is no need to split the infinitive ("to . . . replace"). Choice B is incorrect also because of lack of gerund balance. Choice C is correct. Choice D is incorrect because of lack of gerund balance and because of awkwardness. Choice E is incorrect because of awkwardness.

38. **(A)** Choice A is correct. If you are questioning the singularity of the possessive pronoun-adjective "his," it is correct. The subject of the sentence consists of a singular compound subject, "the sales manager and personnel director." If we wanted to indicate plurality here, we would have to insert the article "the" before the second member ("personnel director") of the compound subject. Choice B is incorrect because "their" must refer to a plural antecedent. Choice C is incorrect because it changes the meaning of the original sentence. Choice D is awkward. Choice E is too wordy.

39. **(B)** Choice A is incorrect because it does not parallel the structure of "not only because of its beauty." Choice B is correct. Choices C, D, and E are incorrect for the same reason that Choice A is incorrect — the lack of parallel structure. Moreover, Choice C is incorrect because "on account" cannot be used as a subordinate conjunction.

40. **(E)** The past participle "known" must modify the subject of the sentence. Choices A and C are, therefore, incorrect because the subject must be "grandfather" — he is the one (not "friends") that is "known to every man, woman, and child in the town." Choice B changes the meaning of the original sentence. Choice D has a double negative ("never . . . no . . ."). Choice E is correct.

41. **(B)** Choice A is incorrect since the correct expression is "no sooner . . . than . . ." Choice B is correct. Choices C, D, and E are incorrect because we must have the "no sooner . . . than" construction.

42. **(A)** Choice A is correct. Choice B is incorrect for two reasons: (1) We use the adverb "so" instead of "as" in a negative comparison; (2) "like" may not be used instead of "as" in this type of comparison. Choice C is awkward. Choice D is roundabout. Choice E changes the meaning of the original sentence.

43. **(C)** The problem in this question is the correct placement of the modifier. The prepositional phrase "much to our disgust" is an adverbial phrase showing result. The phrase, therefore modifies the verb "had been sold out." Accordingly, the phrase should, in this sentence, follow right after the verb it modifies. Choice C, therefore, is correct and the other choices are incorrect. Choice D, incidentally, is incorrect for another reason — it is illogical: the sold-out tickets are obviously disposed of when they are sold out.

44. **(C)** Choice A is incorrect because in this sentence "also" means the same as "in addition." Choice B is awkward. Choice C is correct as a subordinate clause which parallels the preceding subordinate clause. Choice D creates a run-on sentence. Choice E is too wordy.

45. **(C)** Choices A, B, and D are incorrect because of the use of "him joining." The word "joining" is a gerund in this sentence. Its possessive pronoun-adjective must be "his" — not "him." Choice B, moreover, has the unidiomatic expression "objection on." Choice C is correct. Choice E changes the meaning of the original sentence.

46. **(D)** The expression "one another" refers to three or more; "each other" refers to two only. Therefore, Choices A and B are incorrect and Choice D is correct. Choice C is awkward. Choice E changes the meaning of the original sentence.

47. **(E)** The past contrary-to-fact conditional form is "had seen." Therefore, Choices A, B, C, and D are all incorrect. Choice E is correct. Moreover, Choice C has the wrong tense and the wrong tense sequence.

48. **(C)** A misplaced modifier may create a very embarrassing situation — so we can observe in the original sentence. We certainly don't want the fiancé wearing a sheer blouse. Such a blouse clearly belongs on the female. Choices A and D are, therefore, incorrect. Choice B is incorrect because it may appear that the concert is wearing the sheer blouse. Choice C is, of course, correct. Choice E is not acceptable because (1) the phrase "wearing a sheer blouse" is a "squinting" modifier, and (2) the sentence would be inappropriately poetic.

49. **(D)** We are looking for *balanced construction* in this question. Note that the correct Choice D gives us a balanced infinitive construction: "to advise," "(to) transmit", and "(to) supervise." None of the other choices offers this balanced construction.

50. **(A)** Choice A is correct. Choices B and C are incorrect because Frazier did not "own" the decision — it was rendered by the judges and the referee. Choice D is too roundabout. Choice E changes the meaning of the original sentence — and it is too roundabout.

What to Do Now to Improve Your Standard Written English Score

1. Determine your Scaled Score by referring to the Raw Score/Scaled Score Table on the next page.

2. Eliminate your weaknesses by doing the following:

   a. Go over carefully the explanatory answers (page 19) for each of your incorrect answers and for each of your correctly guessed answers.

   b. Study the "Grammar and Usage Refresher" beginning on page 99.

3. Then proceed to Practice Test 2.

4. Repeat the foregoing procedure for Practice Tests 3, 4, and 5.

RAW SCORE/SCALED SCORE TABLE FOR CONVERTING YOUR PRACTICE TEST RAW SCORE TO YOUR SCALED SCORE

When the College Entrance Examination Board sends you your SAT test results, you will get three separate scores:

Verbal Score (from 200 to 800)

Math Score (from 200 to 800)

Standard Written English Score (from 20 to 80)

These scores are your so-called Scaled Scores.

The Standard Written English Scaled Score enables colleges to identify which entering students need additional help in standard English. Accordingly, the Scaled Score that you get on your Standard Written English test will be used by your college-to-be to decide which is the best freshman English course for you.

This Scaled Score is derived by a statistical process from the Raw Score. The Raw Score is the number of items you answered correctly minus $\frac{1}{4}$ of the number of items you answered incorrectly. A Scaled Score of 50 is equivalent to a 50th percentile ranking — that is, about half of those taking the test scored better than you and half scored below you.

The following unofficial Raw Score/Scaled Score Table will give you a rough idea of what your Scaled Score should be for the Standard Written English Practice Test which you have just taken.

Standard Written English Score Table

RAW SCORE*	SCALED SCORE	RAW SCORE*	SCALED SCORE
50	80	33	57.5
49	79	32	55
48	78.5	31	52.5
47	78	30	50
46	77.5	29	48
45	77	28	46
44	76	27	44
43	75	26	42
42	74	25	40
41	73	24	38
40	72	23	36
39	71	22	34
38	70	21	32
37	67.5	20	30
36	65	19	28
35	62.5	18	26
34	60	17	25
		16 *and below*	24 *and below*

*After $\frac{1}{4}$ of the number of incorrect answers has been deducted from the number of correct answers.

Practice Test 2 ⟶

USE THIS SHEET FOR YOUR ANSWERS
PRACTICE TEST 2

	A B C D E		A B C D E		A B C D E		A B C D E		A B C D E
1	☐☐☐☐☐	11	☐☐☐☐☐	21	☐☐☐☐☐	31	☐☐☐☐☐	41	☐☐☐☐☐
2	☐☐☐☐☐	12	☐☐☐☐☐	22	☐☐☐☐☐	32	☐☐☐☐☐	42	☐☐☐☐☐
3	☐☐☐☐☐	13	☐☐☐☐☐	23	☐☐☐☐☐	33	☐☐☐☐☐	43	☐☐☐☐☐
4	☐☐☐☐☐	14	☐☐☐☐☐	24	☐☐☐☐☐	34	☐☐☐☐☐	44	☐☐☐☐☐
5	☐☐☐☐☐	15	☐☐☐☐☐	25	☐☐☐☐☐	35	☐☐☐☐☐	45	☐☐☐☐☐
6	☐☐☐☐☐	16	☐☐☐☐☐	26	☐☐☐☐☐	36	☐☐☐☐☐	46	☐☐☐☐☐
7	☐☐☐☐☐	17	☐☐☐☐☐	27	☐☐☐☐☐	37	☐☐☐☐☐	47	☐☐☐☐☐
8	☐☐☐☐☐	18	☐☐☐☐☐	28	☐☐☐☐☐	38	☐☐☐☐☐	48	☐☐☐☐☐
9	☐☐☐☐☐	19	☐☐☐☐☐	29	☐☐☐☐☐	39	☐☐☐☐☐	49	☐☐☐☐☐
10	☐☐☐☐☐	20	☐☐☐☐☐	30	☐☐☐☐☐	40	☐☐☐☐☐	50	☐☐☐☐☐

Note: At the actual test you will be given an Answer Sheet very much like this sheet in order to record your answers. In doing the following Practice Test, you may prefer to use this Practice Test Answer Sheet. It may, however, be more convenient for you to mark your answer right next to each question. For this method of recording answers, an answer space is, as you will see, provided with each question in this Practice Test.

Standard Written English Practice Test 2

Time: 30 Minutes for the Entire Test

SECTION ONE: GRAMMAR AND USAGE

Directions: In each question, you will find a sentence with four words (or phrases) underlined. In some sentences one of the underlined words (or phrases) is incorrect in the light of the rules of standard written English for grammar, correct usage, and choice of words. No sentence has more than one error. You are to assume that the rest of the sentence (whatever is not underlined) is correct. If you find an error, choose the letter (A *or* B *or* C *or* D) of that underlined word (or phrase) which is incorrect. If you find no error, fill in answer space E.

1. The reason her and her cousin decided to take the train instead of
       A   B

   the plane was that there was a forecast over the radio about an
                 C

   impending storm. No error.
     D   E

   1 A B C D E ☐ ☐ ☐ ☐ ☐

2. Though Seaver pitched real well, the Orioles scored four runs in
     A   B   C

   the ninth inning as a result of two Met errors. No error.
             D   E

   2 A B C D E ☐ ☐ ☐ ☐ ☐

3. Jim and him, after spending several hours trying to ascertain the
          A

   whereabouts of the missing children, finally discovered them in
     B   C

   their aunt's house. No error.
       D   E

   3 A B C D E ☐ ☐ ☐ ☐ ☐

4. After the critics see the two plays, they will, as a result of their
     A   B   C

   experience and background, be able to judge which is the most ef-
                                   D

   fective and moving. No error.
             E

   4 A B C D E ☐ ☐ ☐ ☐ ☐

5. Each of the hotel's 500 rooms were equipped with high quality
           A   B   C

   air conditioning and television. No error.
     D   E

   5 A B C D E ☐ ☐ ☐ ☐ ☐

6. A textbook <u>used</u> in a college class <u>usually always</u> <u>contains</u> an in-
      A   B   C
troduction, a glossary, and <u>an annotated</u> bibliography. <u>No error.</u>
                                          D   E

6 A B C D E
   ⬜ ⬜ ⬜ ⬜ ⬜

7. <u>On</u> any <u>given</u> weekend—especially holiday <u>weekends</u>—the number
    A   B   C
of highway deaths <u>is</u> predictable. <u>No error.</u>
                         D   E

7 A B C D E
   ⬜ ⬜ ⬜ ⬜ ⬜

8. The <u>youth</u> of today are <u>seemingly</u> more sophisticated than were
          A   B
<u>they're</u> parents <u>at</u> the corresponding age. <u>No error.</u>
    C   D   E

8 A B C D E
   ⬜ ⬜ ⬜ ⬜ ⬜

9. The sun <u>hadn't hardly</u> set when the mosquitoes began <u>to sting</u> so
                    A   B
<u>annoyingly</u> that we had to <u>run off</u> from the picnic grounds. <u>No error.</u>
    C   D   E

9 A B C D E
   ⬜ ⬜ ⬜ ⬜ ⬜

10. The lilacs in my <u>Uncle Joe's</u> garden smell <u>sweetly</u> <u>at</u> this time
                          A   B   C
<u>of the year.</u> <u>No error.</u>
      D   E

10 A B C D E
    ⬜ ⬜ ⬜ ⬜ ⬜

11. A wise <u>and</u> experienced administrator <u>will assign</u> a job to <u>whomever</u>
              A   B   C
is <u>best qualified.</u> <u>No error.</u>
      D   E

11 A B C D E
    ⬜ ⬜ ⬜ ⬜ ⬜

12. <u>Being that</u> the United States has a food surplus, it is <u>hard to see</u>
        A   B
why <u>anyone</u> in our country <u>should go</u> hungry. <u>No error.</u>
          C   D   E

12 A B C D E
    ⬜ ⬜ ⬜ ⬜ ⬜

13. <u>Unless</u> there can be some assurance of increased pay, factory <u>morale,</u>
        A   B
<u>all ready</u> low, will collapse <u>completely.</u> <u>No error.</u>
    C   D   E

13 A B C D E
    ⬜ ⬜ ⬜ ⬜ ⬜

14. A series of debates between the major candidates were scheduled
    <u>A</u>   <u>B</u>   <u>C</u>

    for the Labor Day weekend. No error.   14 A B C D E
              <u>D</u>   <u>E</u>

15. As she was small, her huge eyes and her long black hair were neither
    <u>   A   </u>   <u>B</u>   <u>C</u>

    outstanding or attractive. No error.   15 A B C D E
               <u>D</u>   <u>E</u>

16. We did the job as good as we could; however, it did not turn out to
       <u>A</u>   <u>B</u>   <u>C</u>   <u>D</u>

    be satisfactory. No error.   16 A B C D E
              <u>E</u>

17. If we are given the opportunity to stage a play, whose to decide
       <u>A</u>   <u>B</u>   <u>C</u>

    which play we shall produce? No error.   17 A B C D E
              <u>D</u>   <u>E</u>

18. If I would have had more time, I would have written a much more
       <u>A</u>   <u>B</u>   <u>C</u>

    interesting and a far more thorough report. No error.   18 A B C D E
                  <u>D</u>   <u>E</u>

19. More leisure, as well as an abundance of goods, are attainable through
                 <u>A</u>   <u>B</u>   <u>C</u>   <u>D</u>

    automation. No error.   19 A B C D E
              <u>E</u>

20. Morphine and other narcotic drugs are valuable medically; if mis-
                       <u>A</u>   <u>B</u>

    used, however, it can cause irreparable damage. No error.   20 A B C D E
              <u>C</u>   <u>D</u>   <u>E</u>

21. An old miser who picked up yellow pieces of gold had something
                           <u>A</u>   <u>B</u>

    of the simple ardor of a child who picks out yellow flowers. No error.   21 A B C D E
       <u>C</u>   <u>D</u>   <u>E</u>

22. If we here in America cannot live peaceably and happily together,
       A B C
we cannot hope that nations which have different living conditions
— different economic standards, different aspirations, different
mores, different interests — to live peaceably with us. No error.
 D E

22 A B C D E

23. Although Marilyn was not invited to the wedding, she would
       A B
very much have liked to have gone. No error.
 C D E

23 A B C D E

24. Every man, woman, and child in this community are now aware of
       A B
the terrible consequences of the habit of smoking. No error.
 C D E

24 A B C D E

25. The inexperienced teacher had difficulty in controlling the students
whom she was escorting on a visit to the chemical factory, because
 A B
it stunk so. No error.
 C D E

25 A B C D E

26. The question arises as to who should go out this morning in this
       A B C
below-zero weather to clean the snow from the garage entrance, you
or me. No error.
 D E

26 A B C D E

27. Since I loved her very much when she was alive, I prize my
       A
mother's-in-law picture and I wouldn't sell it for all the money in
 B C D
the world. No error.
 E

27 A B C D E

28. Had I have been in my brother's position, I would have hung up
 A B C
the phone in the middle of the conversation. No error.
 D E

28 A B C D E

29. Lie detectors measure physiological changes in respiration, perspira-
    <u>A</u>   <u>B</u>   <u>C</u>

    tion, blood pressure, and muscular grip. No error.
          <u>D</u>   <u>E</u>

29 A B C D E
  ☐ ☐ ☐ ☐ ☐

30. The company is planning a series of lectures for their executives
                              <u>A</u>   <u>B</u>

    so that they may be aware of how to deal with racial problems that
    <u>C</u>

    may occur from time to time. No error.
          <u>D</u>   <u>E</u>

30 A B C D E
  ☐ ☐ ☐ ☐ ☐

SECTION TWO: SENTENCE CORRECTION

Directions: Each sentence is partly or wholly underlined. In some cases, what is underlined is correct — in other cases, it is incorrect. The five choices that follow each sentence represent various ways of writing the underlined part. Choice A is the same as the original underlining but Choices B, C, D, and E are different. If, in your judgment, the original sentence is better than any of the changed sentences, select Choice A. If another choice produces the only correct sentence, select that other choice (B or C or D or E).

In making your choice, you should observe the rules of standard written English. Your choice must fulfill the requirements of correct grammar, diction (word choice), sentence structure, and punctuation.

If a choice changes the meaning of the original sentence, do not make that choice.

31. <u>Tricia Nixon was just engaged and was born on St. Patrick's Day.</u>

   (A) Tricia Nixon was just engaged and was born on St. Patrick's Day.
   (B) Tricia Nixon was just engaged, she was born on St. Patrick's Day.
   (C) On St. Patrick's Day Tricia Nixon was born, she was just engaged.
   (D) Tricia Nixon, born on St. Patrick's Day, was just engaged.
   (E) Tricia Nixon was engaged and she was born on St. Patrick's Day.

A B C D E
31 ☐ ☐ ☐ ☐ ☐

32. As no one knows the truth <u>as fully as him, no one but him</u> can provide the testimony needed to clear the accused of the very serious charges.

   (A) as fully as him, no one but him
   (B) as fully as he, no one but him
   (C) as fully as he, no one but he
   (D) as fully as he does, no one but he
   (E) as fully as he does, no one but he alone

A B C D E
32 ☐ ☐ ☐ ☐ ☐

33. After the defendant charged him with being prejudiced, the judge withdrew from the case.

    (A) After the defendant charged him with being prejudiced
    (B) On account of the defendant charged him with being prejudiced
    (C) Charging the defendant with being prejudiced
    (D) Upon the defendant charging him with being prejudiced
    (E) The defendant charged him with being prejudiced

    A B C D E
33 ☐ ☐ ☐ ☐ ☐

34. Although the mourners differed in color and in dress, they all sat silently together for an hour to honor Whitney M. Young Jr.

    (A) Although the mourners differed in color and in dress
    (B) Because the mourners differed in color and in dress
    (C) The mourners having differed in color and in dress
    (D) When the mourners differed in color and in dress
    (E) The mourners differed in color and in dress

    A B C D E
34 ☐ ☐ ☐ ☐ ☐

35. To avoid the hot sun, our plans were that we would travel at night.

    (A) To avoid the hot sun, our plans were that we would travel at night.
    (B) To try to avoid the hot sun, our plans were for travel at night.
    (C) Our plans were night travel so that we could avoid the hot sun.
    (D) We planned to travel at night, that's how we would avoid the hot sun.
    (E) To avoid the hot sun, we made plans to travel at night.

    A B C D E
35 ☐ ☐ ☐ ☐ ☐

36. Whatever she had any thoughts about, they were interrupted as the hotel lobby door opened.

    (A) Whatever she had any thoughts about
    (B) Whatever her thoughts
    (C) Whatever be her thoughts
    (D) What her thoughts were
    (D) What thoughts

    A B C D E
36 ☐ ☐ ☐ ☐ ☐

37. The use of radar, as well as the two-way radio, make it possible for state troopers to intercept most speeders.

    (A) make it possible
    (B) makes it possible
    (C) allows the possibility
    (D) makes possible
    (E) make it a possibility

    A B C D E
37 ☐ ☐ ☐ ☐ ☐

38. Irregardless what reasons or excuses are offered, there is only one word for his behavior: cowardice.

    (A) Irregardless what reasons or excuses are offered
    (B) Regardless about what reasons or excuses he may offer
    (C) Since he offered reasons and excuses
    (D) Nevertheless he offered reasons and excuses
    (E) No matter what reasons and excuses are offered

    A B C D E
38 ☐ ☐ ☐ ☐ ☐

39. <u>What a man cannot state, he does not perfectly know.</u>

    (A) What a man cannot state, he does not perfectly know.
    (B) A man cannot state if he does not perfectly know.
    (C) A man cannot perfectly know if he does not state.
    (D) That which a man cannot state is that which he cannot perfectly know.
    (E) What a man cannot state is the reason he does not perfectly know.

                                                                                                      A B C D E
                                                                                                     39 ⬜ ⬜ ⬜ ⬜ ⬜

40. Professional writers realize that <u>they cannot hope to effect</u> the reader precisely as they wish without care and practice in the use of words.

    (A) they cannot hope to effect
    (B) they cannot hope to have an effect on
    (C) they cannot hope to affect
    (D) they cannot hope effecting
    (E) they cannot try to affect

                                                                                                                      A B C D E
                                                                                                     40 ⬜ ⬜ ⬜ ⬜ ⬜

41. I've met two men <u>whom, I believe,</u> were policemen.

    (A) whom, I believe,
    (B) who, I believe
    (C) each, I believe,
    (D) and I believe they
    (E) who

                                                                                                                     A B C D E
                                                                                                     41 ⬜ ⬜ ⬜ ⬜ ⬜

42. Such people <u>never have and never will be trusted.</u>

    (A) never have and never will be trusted
    (B) never have and will be trusted
    (C) never have trusted and never will trust
    (D) never have been trusted and never will be trusted
    (E) never have had anyone trust them and never will have anyone trust them

                                                                                                                     A B C D E
                                                                                                     42 ⬜ ⬜ ⬜ ⬜ ⬜

43. Your employer would have been inclined to favor your request <u>if you would have waited for an occasion</u> when he was less busy.

    (A) if you would have waited for an occasion
    (B) if you would only have waited for an occasion
    (C) if you were to have waited for an occasion
    (D) if you waited for an occasion
    (E) if you had waited for an occasion

                                                                                                                     A B C D E
                                                                                                     43 ⬜ ⬜ ⬜ ⬜ ⬜

44. I find Henry James' prose style more difficult to read than James Joyce.

    (A) I find Henry James' prose style more difficult to read than James Joyce.

    (B) I find Henry Jame's prose style more difficult to read than James Joyce'.

    (C) I find Henry James's prose style more difficult to read than James Joyce's.

    (D) I find the prose style of Henry James more difficult to read than James Joyce.

    (E) Henry James' prose style I find more difficult to read than I find James Joyce.

    A B C D E
44 ☐ ☐ ☐ ☐ ☐

45. Neither Dr. Conant nor his followers knows what to do about the problem.

    (A) Neither Dr. Conant nor his followers knows what to do about the problem.

    (B) Neither Dr. Conant or his followers knows what to do about the problem.

    (C) Neither Dr. Conant nor his followers know what to do about the problem.

    (D) Neither Dr. Conant nor his followers knows what to do as far as the problem goes.

    (E) As to the problem, neither Dr. Conant nor his followers knows what to do.

    A B C D E
45 ☐ ☐ ☐ ☐ ☐

46. Although I know this house and this neighborhood as well as I know myself, and although my friend here seems not hardly to know them at all, nevertheless he has lived here longer than I.

    (A) and although my friend here here seems not hardly to know them at all.

    (B) and even though my friend here seems hardly to know them at all

    (C) and in spite of the fact that my friend doesn't hardly seem to know them at all

    (D) and because my friend here hardly seems to know them at all

    (E) my friend here seems hardly to know them at all

    A B C D E
46 ☐ ☐ ☐ ☐ ☐

47. So I leave it with all of you: Which came out of the open door — the lady or the tiger.

    (A) the lady or the tiger.
    (B) the lady or the Tiger!
    (C) the Tiger or the lady.
    (D) the Lady or the tiger.
    (E) the lady or the tiger?

    A B C D E
47 ☐ ☐ ☐ ☐ ☐

48. The machine is not easy to fool, <u>it isn't altogether foolproof either.</u>

    (A) it isn't altogether foolproof either
    (B) or is it foolproof
    (C) and it isn't completely fooled by anyone
    (D) nor is it entirely foolproof
    (E) so it isn't altogether foolproof

                                  A B C D E
                                48 ☐ ☐ ☐ ☐ ☐

49. The police and agents of the F.B.I. <u>arrested the owner of a Madison Avenue art gallery yesterday</u> and charged him with receiving paintings stolen last November.

    (A) arrested the owner of a Madison Avenue art gallery yesterday
    (B) yesterday arrested the owner of a Madison Avenue art gallery
    (C) arrested the owner yesterday of a Madison Avenue art gallery
    (D) had the owner of a Madison Avenue art gallery yesterday arrested
    (E) arranged the arrest yesterday of a Madison Avenue art gallery owner

                                  A B C D E
                                49 ☐ ☐ ☐ ☐ ☐

50. At the end of the play about women's liberation, the leading lady cautioned the audience not to judge womanhood by the way <u>she dresses.</u>

    (A) she dresses
    (B) she dressed
    (C) they dress
    (D) they dressed
    (E) it dresses

                                  A B C D E
                                50 ☐ ☐ ☐ ☐ ☐

NOW THAT YOU HAVE COMPLETED PRACTICE TEST 2

1. Turn to the Answer Key on page 38.

2. How many **correct answers** do you have out of 50 questions? ....

3. How many **incorrect answers** do you have out of 50 questions? ....

4. Deduct ¼ of the number of incorrect answers from the number of correct answers to get a **"raw score"** of ....

5. Your **"scaled score"** for this test, according to the Raw Score/Scaled Score Table on page 24 is ....

ANSWER KEY FOR PRACTICE TEST 2

1. A	11. C	21. E	31. D	41. B
2. B	12. A	22. D	32. B	42. D
3. A	13. C	23. D	33. A	43. E
4. D	14. C	24. B	34. A	44. C
5. B	15. D	25. C	35. E	45. C
6. B	16. B	26. D	36. B	46. B
7. E	17. C	27. B	37. B	47. E
8. C	18. A	28. A	38. E	48. D
9. A	19. C	29. E	39. A	49. B
10. B	20. C	30. B	40. C	50. E

EXPLANATORY ANSWERS
FOR PRACTICE TEST 2

1. **(A)** "The reason *she* and her cousin . . ."
The subject form of the personal pronoun is *she*—not *her*.

2. **(B)** "Though Seaver pitched *really* well . . ."
The adverb *well* must be modified by another adverb such as *really*—not by an adjective such as *real*.

3. **(A)** "Jim and *he* . . . finally discovered . . ."
Jim and *he* are the compound subjects of the verb *discovered*. The subject form of the pronoun is *he*—not *him*.

4. **(D)** ". . . the *more* effective and moving."
In a comparison of two things (such as two plays), we use the comparative degree (*more*)—not the superlative degree (*most*).

5. **(B)** "Each of the hotel's 500 rooms *was* equipped . . ."
The singular subject (*Each*) requires a singular verb (*was equipped*—not *were equipped*).

6. **(B)** "A textbook . . . usually contains . . ."
One cannot use the two words *usually* and *always* together because one word contradicts the other. *Usually* means almost all the time; *always* means all the time.

7. **(E)** All underlined parts are correct.

8. **(C)** ". . . than were *their* parents . . ."
The possessive adjective *their* modifies the noun *parents*. The contraction *they're* means *they are*.

9. **(A)** "The sun *had hardly* set . . ."
The expression *hadn't hardly* is always incorrect.

10. **(B)** "The lilacs . . . smell *sweet* . . ."
We use the predicate adjective (*sweet*) after the copulative verb (*smell*). The use of the adverb *sweetly* is incorrect in this case.

11. **(C)** ". . . to *whoever* is best qualified."
Since the underlined word is the subject of the subordinate clause, *whoever* (the nomina-tive form) must be used. *Whomever* is the objective form.

12. **(A)** "*Since* the United States has a food surplus . . ."
Being that is always incorrect for *since* or *because*.

13. **(C)** ". . . factory morale, *already* low . . ."
All ready means everybody (is) ready. The adverb *already* modifying the adjective *low* is correct here.

14. **(C)** "A series of debates . . . *was* scheduled . . ."
Series is a collective noun with a feeling of singularity. As a singular subject, it takes a singular verb (*was scheduled*).

15. **(D)** ". . . neither outstanding *nor* attractive."
The correlative conjunctions are *neither* . . . *nor*—not *neither* . . . *or*.

16. **(B)** "We did the job as *well* as we could . . ."
The adverb *well* must be used to modify the verb *did*. The adjective *good* is incorrect for such modification.

17. **(C)** ". . . *who's* to decide . . ."
The interrogative pronoun-adjective *whose* should not be used here. We mean: *who is* (*who's*).

18. **(A)** "If I *had had* more time . . ."
In a contrary to fact condition in the past, the "if clause" must have a past perfect subjunctive form (*had had*).

19. **(C)** "More leisure . . . *is* attainable . . ."
Since the subject (*leisure*) is singular, the verb must be singular (*is attainable*).

20. **(C)** ". . . *they* can cause irreparable damage."
We have a plural subject: *Morphine* and *drugs*. Accordingly, the pronoun which occurs later in the sentence must be plural (*they*) since a pronoun must agree with its antecedent in number.

The verb in this past conditional situation should be *had been* — not *had have been*. Another way of correctly starting the sentence would be "If I had been..."

21. **(E)** All underlined parts are correct.

22. **(D)** "... we cannot hope that nations ... *will live* peaceably with us."
The clause beginning with *that nations* ... requires a finite verb *(will live)* — not an infinitive *(to live)*.

23. **(D)** "... she would very much have liked *to go*." A present infinitive *(to go)* — not a past infinitive *(to have gone)* is used after a verb which is in the perfect tense *(would have liked)*.

24. **(B)** "... *is* now aware of ..."
A compound subject *(man, woman, and child)* which is introduced by *every* must have a singular verb *(is* now aware — not *are* now aware).

25. **(C)** "... because it *stank* so."
The past tense of the verb *stink* is *stank* — not *stunk*. The present perfect tense, however, is *has stunk*.

26. **(D)** "... you or *I*."
A pronoun which is an appositive of a subject must, like the subject, be in the nominative case. The word *who* is the subject of the clause "who should go out..." The subject of a clause or a sentence is in the nominative case. The pronouns which act as appositives to the subject must, accordingly, have nominative case forms *(you and I* — not *you and me)*.

27. **(B)** "I prize my *mother-in-law's* picture..." When you form the possessive of a compound word, you must add the *apostrophe* and *s* only to the last word in the compound.

28. **(A)** "Had I *been* in my brother's position ..."

29. **(E)** All underlined parts are correct.

30. **(B)** "The company is planning a series of lectures for *its* executives..."
A singular pronoun-adjective *(its* — not *their)* must be used to refer to a collective noun *(company)* when the members of the collective noun are considered as a unit.

31. **(D)** The important thing is that Tricia Nixon had (finally) become engaged. Choice D, alone, brings out the primary importance of the engagement and the secondary importance of her being born on St. Patrick's Day. Moreover, Choices B and C are run-on sentences.

32. **(B)** Choice A is incorrect because the nominative form ("he") is required: "as fully as him" is wrong. Choice B is correct. Choices C, D, and E are incorrect because the object of the preposition must have an objective case form — the preposition "but" must be followed by the object case form "him."

33. **(A)** Choice A is correct. Choice B is incorrect because "on account" may not be used as a subordinate conjunction. Choice C is incorrect because it gives the meaning that the judge is doing the charging. Choice D is incorrect because the possessive noun ("defendant") modifying the gerund ("charging") must take the form "defendant's." Choice E creates a run-on sentence.

34. **(A)** Choice A is correct. Choices B, C, and D are incorrect because they change the meaning of the original sentence. Choice E creates a run-on sentence.

35. **(E)** Choices A and B are incorrect because they give the idea that the plans are trying to avoid the hot sun. Choice C is awkward. Choice D is a run-on sentence. Choice E is correct.

36. **(B)** Choice A is too wordy. Choice B is correct. Choice C is incorrect because it changes the tense of the original sentence — "Whatever (may) be her thoughts" is in the present tense. Choice D does not retain the meaning of the original sentence. Choice E makes no sense.

37. **(B)** Choices A and E are incorrect because the subject word "use" requires a singular verb ("makes"). Choice B is correct. Choices C and D are awkward.

38. **(E)** "Irregardless" (Choice A) is incorrect. "Regardless about" (Choice B) is unidiomatic. Choices C and D change the meaning of the original sentence. Moreover, Choice D makes the sentence ungrammatical. Choice E is correct.

39. **(A)** Choice A is correct. Choices B, C, and E change the meaning of the original sentence. Choice D is too wordy.

40. **(C)** The infinitive "to effect" means "to bring about" — this is not the meaning intended in the original sentence. Therefore. Choices A, B, and D are incorrect. Choice C is correct. Choice E changes the meaning of the original sentence.

41. **(B)** In the original sentence, "who" should replace "whom" as the subject of the subordinate clause ("who were policemen"). "I believe" is simply a parenthetical expression. Therefore, Choice A is incorrect and Choice B is correct. Choice C creates a run-on sentence. Choice D improperly changes the sentence from a complex type to a compound type. Choice E does not retain the meaning of the original sentence.

42. **(D)** Choices A and B suffer from improper ellipsis. Choice C changes the meaning of the original sentence. Choice D is correct. Choice E is too wordy.

43. **(E)** Sequence of tenses in a past contrary -to fact condition requires the "had waited" form in the "if" clause. Therefore Choices A, B, C, and D are incorrect and Choice E is correct.

44. **(C)** We are concerned here with the apostrophe use with a singular name ending in "s." We are also concerned with improper ellipsis. In Choice A, "James'" is correct but we must either say "to read than *the prose style* of James Joyce" or "to read than James Joyce's." In Choice B, "Jame's" is incorrect — his name is not "Jame." Choice C is correct. Choices D and E are incorrect for the same reason that Choice A is incorrect — improper ellipsis.

45. **(C)** Choice A is incorrect because in a "neither..nor" construction, the number of the verb is determined by the "nor" subject noun ("followers"). Since "followers" is plural, the verb must be plural ("know"). Choices B, D, and E are incorrect for the same reason. Moreover, Choice B is incorrect for another reason: the correlative form is "neither...nor" — not "neither...or". Choice C is correct.

46. **(B)** Avoid the double negative. Choices A and C suffer from the double negative fault. Choice B is correct. Choice D changes the meaning of the original sentence. Choice E creates a run-on sentence.

47. **(E)** The original sentence is interrogative. Accordingly, the sentence must end with a question mark. Choice E is correct.

48. **(D)** Choice A is incorrect because it creates a run-on sentence. Choice B fails to include the all-inclusive ("altogether," "completely," "entirely") idea of the original sentence. Choice C changes the meaning of the original sentence. Choice D is correct. Choice E changes the meaning of the original sentence.

49. **(B)** The adverb "yesterday" should, in this sentence, be placed before the modified verb ("arrested"). Therefore, Choices A and C are incorrect and Choice B is correct. Choices D and E are too roundabout.

50. **(E)** The singular historical present tense should be used here. Reasons: (1) a general truth is being expressed — this requires the present tense; (2) "womanhood" is singular. Also, the personal pronoun "it" must be used since its antecedent is "womanhood" — an abstract noun. Therefore Choice E is correct and all the other choices are incorrect.

Practice Test 3 $\longrightarrow$

USE THIS SHEET FOR YOUR ANSWERS
PRACTICE TEST 3

	A B C D E		A B C D E		A B C D E		A B C D E		A B C D E
1	☐ ☐ ☐ ☐ ☐	11	☐ ☐ ☐ ☐ ☐	21	☐ ☐ ☐ ☐ ☐	31	☐ ☐ ☐ ☐ ☐	41	☐ ☐ ☐ ☐ ☐
2	☐ ☐ ☐ ☐ ☐	12	☐ ☐ ☐ ☐ ☐	22	☐ ☐ ☐ ☐ ☐	32	☐ ☐ ☐ ☐ ☐	42	☐ ☐ ☐ ☐ ☐
3	☐ ☐ ☐ ☐ ☐	13	☐ ☐ ☐ ☐ ☐	23	☐ ☐ ☐ ☐ ☐	33	☐ ☐ ☐ ☐ ☐	43	☐ ☐ ☐ ☐ ☐
4	☐ ☐ ☐ ☐ ☐	14	☐ ☐ ☐ ☐ ☐	24	☐ ☐ ☐ ☐ ☐	34	☐ ☐ ☐ ☐ ☐	44	☐ ☐ ☐ ☐ ☐
5	☐ ☐ ☐ ☐ ☐	15	☐ ☐ ☐ ☐ ☐	25	☐ ☐ ☐ ☐ ☐	35	☐ ☐ ☐ ☐ ☐	45	☐ ☐ ☐ ☐ ☐
6	☐ ☐ ☐ ☐ ☐	16	☐ ☐ ☐ ☐ ☐	26	☐ ☐ ☐ ☐ ☐	36	☐ ☐ ☐ ☐ ☐	46	☐ ☐ ☐ ☐ ☐
7	☐ ☐ ☐ ☐ ☐	17	☐ ☐ ☐ ☐ ☐	27	☐ ☐ ☐ ☐ ☐	37	☐ ☐ ☐ ☐ ☐	47	☐ ☐ ☐ ☐ ☐
8	☐ ☐ ☐ ☐ ☐	18	☐ ☐ ☐ ☐ ☐	28	☐ ☐ ☐ ☐ ☐	38	☐ ☐ ☐ ☐ ☐	48	☐ ☐ ☐ ☐ ☐
9	☐ ☐ ☐ ☐ ☐	19	☐ ☐ ☐ ☐ ☐	29	☐ ☐ ☐ ☐ ☐	39	☐ ☐ ☐ ☐ ☐	49	☐ ☐ ☐ ☐ ☐
10	☐ ☐ ☐ ☐ ☐	20	☐ ☐ ☐ ☐ ☐	30	☐ ☐ ☐ ☐ ☐	40	☐ ☐ ☐ ☐ ☐	50	☐ ☐ ☐ ☐ ☐

Note: At the actual test you will be given an Answer Sheet very much like this sheet in order to record your answers. In doing the following Practice Test, you may prefer to use this Practice Test Answer Sheet. It may, however, be more convenient for you to mark your answer right next to each question. For this method of recording answers, an answer space is, as you will see, provided with each question in this Practice Test.

Standard Written English
Practice Test 3

Time: 30 Minutes for the Entire Test

SECTION ONE: GRAMMAR AND USAGE

Directions: In each question, you will find a sentence with four words (or phrases) underlined. In some sentences one of the underlined words (or phrases) is incorrect in the light of the rules of standard written English for grammar, correct usage, and choice of words. No sentence has more than one error. You are to assume that the rest of the sentence (whatever is not underlined) is correct. If you find an error, choose the letter (A *or* B *or* C *or* D) of that underlined word (or phrase) which is incorrect. If you find no error, fill in answer space E.

1. We were terrified by sounds: the screaming of the wind; the rest-
   A   B
   less rustle of leaves in the trees; and the sudden, overwhelming ex-
        C   D
   plosions of thunder. No error.
                        E

   A B C D E
   1 ⍿ ⍿ ⍿ ⍿ ⍿

2. His dog having barked a warning, the watchman who
              A
   had been assigned to guard the valuable truckload of chemicals
        B
   pulled out his gun quick and proceeded to search out a possible
                     C   D
   intruder. No error.
             E

   A B C D E
   2 ⍿ ⍿ ⍿ ⍿ ⍿

3. Your employer would have been inclined to favor your request if
                               A
   you would have waited for an occasion when he was less busy with
        B   C
   other more important matters. No error.
         D   E

   A B C D E
   3 ⍿ ⍿ ⍿ ⍿ ⍿

4. Popular impressions about slang are often erroneous: their is no
                         A   B
   necessary connection, for example, between what is slang and what
                         C   D
   is ungrammatical. No error.
                     E

   A B C D E
   4 ⍿ ⍿ ⍿ ⍿ ⍿

45

5. After all the performers <u>had finished</u> their performances, I knew
A

the winner to be <u>he</u> <u>whom</u> I had singled out <u>the moment</u> I had
B   C   D

met him. <u>No error.</u>
E

```
  A B C D E
5 □ □ □ □ □
```

6. <u>Nor</u> has the writer even the satisfaction of calling his reader a fool
A

for misunderstanding him, since he seldom hears <u>of</u> it; it is the
B

reader who calls the writer a fool <u>for</u> not being able to express
C

<u>hisself.</u> <u>No error.</u>
D   E

```
  A B C D E
6 □ □ □ □ □
```

7. Struggling <u>hard</u> against almost <u>insuperable odds</u>, he was unable,
A   B

<u>to effect</u> even a small change in the <u>course</u> of the vehicle. <u>No error.</u>
C   D   E

```
  A B C D E
7 □ □ □ □ □
```

8. I appreciate <u>you</u> helping me <u>to do</u> the dishes, but I wish you would
A   B

<u>lay</u> them down on the table more <u>carefully.</u> <u>No error.</u>
C   D   E

```
  A B C D E
8 □ □ □ □ □
```

9. Looking through the <u>main gate</u> at the southwest corner of the park
A

where the bridle path <u>emerges</u> from the wood, <u>the blooming lilac</u>
B   C

can be seen in <u>great sprays</u> of purple, lavender, and white. <u>No error.</u>
D   E

```
  A B C D E
9 □ □ □ □ □
```

10. <u>No sooner</u> had be <u>begun</u> to speak <u>when</u> an ominous muttering
A   B   C

<u>arose</u> from the audience. <u>No error.</u>
D   E

```
   A B C D E
10 □ □ □ □ □
```

11. Separate vacations by husband and wife are <u>much esteemed</u> in cer-
A

tain circles, but if such holidays <u>last</u> more than a year <u>or so</u>, even
B   C

the most liberal raise <u>there</u> eyebrows. <u>No error.</u>
D   E

```
   A B C D E
11 □ □ □ □ □
```

12. Proud of his skill in serving liquor, he poured some of the wine
                        A   B
into his own glass first so that he would get the cork
                                      C
and not the lady. No error.
        D   E

12 A B C D E

13. The captain of the squad was a sophomore, one of last year's
                                                              A
freshman team, a player of great intelligence, and, above all,
    B   C
endurance. No error.
    D   E

13 A B C D E

14. Everyone is expected to attend the afternoon session but the field
              A   B   C
supervisor, the sales manager, and I. No error.
                                D   E

14 A B C D E

15. No one who has seen him work in the laboratory can deny that
                  A   B
Williams has an interest and an aptitude for chemical experimenta-
                 C   D
tion. No error.
        E

15 A B C D E

16. Manslaughter is where a person is killed unlawfully but without
                     A   B   C   D
premeditation. No error.
                   E

16 A B C D E

17. The reason teenagers tend to follow the trend while openly declaring
                        A   B
themselves nonconformists is because they are really insecure.
        C   D
No error.
    E

17 A B C D E

18. Its not generally known that the word "buxom" originally came
    A   B   C
from the Old English verb meaning "to bend." No error.
            D   E

18 A B C D E

19. A <u>great many</u> educators <u>firmly</u> believe that English is one of the
      A   B
<u>poorest</u> taught subjects in high school <u>today.</u> <u>No error.</u>
      C   D   E

19 A B C D E
    ☐ ☐ ☐ ☐ ☐

20. Developed by the <u>research</u> engineers of Dupont, <u>the government</u>
                      A   B
considers the new explosive a <u>sure</u> deterrent <u>to war.</u> <u>No error.</u>
                               C   D   E

20 A B C D E
    ☐ ☐ ☐ ☐ ☐

21. Baseball, football, and soccer have <u>all</u> been approved as
                                        A
<u>extracurricular</u> activities. From <u>either</u> of them a coach can earn
      B   C
several <u>hundreds</u> of dollars each season. <u>No error.</u>
          D   E

21 A B C D E
    ☐ ☐ ☐ ☐ ☐

22. After I <u>listened</u> to the violinist and cellist, and enjoyed <u>their</u>
              A   B
interpretations, I <u>hurried</u> home <u>to practice.</u> <u>No error.</u>
                     C   D   E

22 A B C D E
    ☐ ☐ ☐ ☐ ☐

23. Most of the citizens have <u>no doubt</u> that the <u>Mayor taking</u> a firm
                               A   B
stand in the matter <u>of clamping down</u> on drug peddlers will bear
                      C
immediate results in <u>ridding the city</u> of these vermin. <u>No error.</u>
                       D   E

23 A B C D E
    ☐ ☐ ☐ ☐ ☐

24. <u>Having sat</u> the bag of dirty clothes <u>on</u> a bench in the apartment
      A   B
building laundry room, Mrs. Williams <u>chatted</u> with a neighbor
                                        C
until a washing machine <u>was</u> available. <u>No error.</u>
                          D   E

24 A B C D E
    ☐ ☐ ☐ ☐ ☐

25. None of the crew members who <u>flew</u> with me <u>over</u> Hanoi is
                                   A   B
happy today <u>about</u> the destruction <u>caused</u> in that bombing mission.
              C   D
<u>No error.</u>
  E

25 A B C D E
    ☐ ☐ ☐ ☐ ☐

26. It was our neighbor's opinion that if Kennedy was alive today, the
    _____   ____
       A   B
    country would have fewer problems than it has now. No error.
           _____   ____   _____
               C   D   E

    A B C D E
    26 ☐ ☐ ☐ ☐ ☐

27. We, as parents who are interested in the welfare of our son, are
    ___
     A
    strongly opposed to him associating with individuals who
    _____   ___
       B   C
    do not seem to have moral scruples. No error.
    _____   _____
        D   E

    A B C D E
    27 ☐ ☐ ☐ ☐ ☐

28. If anyone in the audience has anything to add to what the speaker
                              ___   _____   ____
                               A   B   3
    has already said, let them speak up. No error.
                        ____   _____
                         D   E

    A B C D E
    28 ☐ ☐ ☐ ☐ ☐

29. It was very nice of the Rodriguezes to invite my husband, my
    __   _____
     A   B
    mother, and I to their New Year's Eve party. No error.
            ___   _____   _____
             C   D   E

    A B C D E
    29 ☐ ☐ ☐ ☐ ☐

30. Neither rain nor snow nor sleet keep the postman from delivering
                 ___   ____   ____
                  A   B   C
    our letters which we so much look forward to receiving. No error.
                                  _____   _____
                                       D   E

    A B C D E
    30 ☐ ☐ ☐ ☐ ☐

SECTION TWO: SENTENCE CORRECTION

Directions: Each sentence is partly or wholly underlined. In some cases, what is underlined is correct — in other cases, it is incorrect. The five choices that follow each sentence represent various ways of writing the underlined part. Choice A is the same as the original underlining but Choices B, C, D, and E are different. If, in your judgment, the original sentence is better than any of the changed sentences, select Choice A. If another choice produces the only correct sentence, select that other choice (B or C or D or E).

In making your choice, you should observe the rules of standard written English. Your choice must fulfill the requirements of correct grammar, diction (word choice), sentence structure, and punctuation.

If a choice changes the meaning of the original sentence, do not make that choice.

31. <u>The students requested a meeting with the chancellor</u> since they desired a greater voice in university policy.

    (A) The students requested a meeting with the chancellor
    (B) A meeting with the chancellor was requested by the students
    (C) It occurred to the students to request a meeting with the chancellor
    (D) The chancellor was the one with whom the students requested a meeting
    (E) The students insisted upon a meeting with the chancellor

    31 A B C D E

32. Three American scientists were jointly awarded the Nobel Prize in Medicine <u>for their study of viruses which led to discoveries.</u>

    (A) for their study of viruses which led to discoveries
    (B) for their discoveries concerning viruses
    (C) as a prize for their discoveries about viruses
    (D) the discovery into viruses being the reason
    (E) for their virus discoveries

    32 A B C D E

33. <u>You must convince me of promptness in returning the money</u> before I can agree to lend you $100.

    (A) You must convince me of promptness in returning the money
    (B) The loan of the money must be returned promptly
    (C) You must understand that you will have to assure me of a prompt money return
    (D) You will have to convince me that you will return the money promptly
    (E) You will return the money promptly

    33 A B C D E

34. Because Bob was an outstanding athlete in high school, <u>in addition to a fine scholastic record,</u> he was awarded a scholarship at Harvard.

    (A) in addition to a fine scholastic record,
    (B) also a student of excellence,
    (C) and had amassed an excellent scholastic record,
    (D) his scholastic record was also outstanding,
    (E) as well as a superior student,

A B C D E
34 ☐ ☐ ☐ ☐ ☐

35. Although pre-season odds against the Mets had been 100 to 1, <u>the Orioles were trounced by them in the World Series.</u>

    (A) the Orioles were trounced by them in the World Series
    (B) the World Series victors were the Mets who trounced the Orioles
    (C) they won the World Series by trouncing the Orioles
    (D) which is hard to believe since the Orioles were trounced in the World Series
    (E) it was the Mets who trounced the Orioles in the World Series

A B C D E
35 ☐ ☐ ☐ ☐ ☐

36. Before you can make a fresh fruit salad, <u>you must buy oranges, bananas, pineapples and peaches are necessary.</u>

    (A) you must buy oranges, bananas, pineapples and peaches are necessary.
    (B) you must buy oranges and bananas and pineapples and peaches.
    (C) you must buy oranges and bananas. And other fruit such as pineapples and peaches.
    (D) you must buy oranges and bananas and other fruit. Such as pineapples and peaches.
    (E) you must buy oranges, bananas, pineapples, and peaches

A B C D E
36 ☐ ☐ ☐ ☐ ☐

37. The physical education department of the school offers instruction <u>to learn how to swim, how to play tennis, and how to defend oneself.</u>

    (A) to learn how to swim, how to play tennis, and how to defend oneself
    (B) in swimming, playing tennis, and protecting oneself
    (C) in regard to how to swim, how to play tennis, and how to protect oneself
    (D) for the purpose of swimming, playing tennis, and protecting oneself
    (E) in swimming, playing tennis, and to protect oneself

A B C D E
37 ☐ ☐ ☐ ☐ ☐

38. <u>Joe couldn't wait for his return to his home</u> after being in the army for two years.

    (A) Joe couldn't wait for his return to his home
    (B) There was a strong desire on Joe's part to return home
    (C) Joe was eager to return home
    (D) Joe wanted home badly
    (E) Joe arranged to return home

A B C D E
38 ☐ ☐ ☐ ☐ ☐

39. Trash, filth, and muck are clogging the streets of the city and <u>that's not all, the sidewalks are full of garbage.</u>

    (A) that's not all, the sidewalks are full of garbage.
    (B) another thing: garbage is all over the sidewalks
    (C) the garbage cans haven't been emptied for days
    (D) in addition, garbage is lying all over the sidewalks
    (E) what's more, the sidewalks have garbage that is lying all over them

        A B C D E
39 0 0 0 0 0

40. Tired and discouraged by the problems of the day, <u>Myra decided to have a good dinner, and then lie down for an hour, and then go dancing.</u>

    (A) Myra decided to have a good dinner, and then lie down for an hour, and then go dancing.
    (B) Myra decided to have a good dinner, lying down for an hour, and then dancing.
    (C) Myra decided to have a good dinner, lie down for an hour, and then dancing.
    (D) Myra decided to have a good dinner, lay down for an hour, and then dance.
    (E) Myra decided to have a good dinner, lie down for an hour, and then go dancing.

        A B C D E
40 0 0 0 0 0

41. I am not certain <u>in respect to which courses</u> to take.

    (A) in respect to which courses
    (B) about which courses
    (C) which courses
    (D) as to the choice of which courses
    (E) for which courses I am

        A B C D E
41 0 0 0 0 0

42. The people of the besieged village had no doubt <u>that the end was drawing near.</u>

    (A) that the end was drawing near
    (B) about the nearness of the end
    (C) it was clear that the end was near
    (D) concerning the end's being near
    (E) that all would die

        A B C D E
42 0 0 0 0 0

43. There isn't a single man among us <u>who is skilled in the art of administering first-aid.</u>

    (A) who is skilled in the art of administering first-aid
    (B) who knows how to administer first-aid
    (C) who knows the administration of first-aid
    (D) who is a first-aid man
    (E) who administers first-aid

        A B C D E
43 0 0 0 0 0

44. This is the hole <u>that was squeezed through by the mouse.</u>

   (A) that was squeezed through by the mouse
   (B) that the mouse was seen to squeeze through
   (C) the mouse squeezed through it
   (D) that the mouse squeezed through
   (E) like what the mouse squeezed through

   A B C D E
   44 ☐ ☐ ☐ ☐ ☐

45. <u>She soundly fell asleep</u> after having finished the novel.

   (A) She soundly fell asleep
   (B) She decided to sleep
   (C) She went on to her sleep
   (D) She fell to sleep
   (E) She fell fast asleep

   A B C D E
   45 ☐ ☐ ☐ ☐ ☐

46. <u>Go where he may,</u> he is the life of the party.

   (A) Go where he may,
   (B) Where he may go,
   (C) Wherever he goes,
   (D) Wherever he may happen to go,
   (E) Whatever he does,

   A B C D E
   46 ☐ ☐ ☐ ☐ ☐

47. At first we were willing to support him, <u>afterwards it occurred to us that</u> he ought to provide for himself.

   (A) afterwards it occurred to us that
   (B) that wasn't the thing to do since
   (C) but we came to realize that
   (D) we came to the conclusion, however, that
   (E) then we decided that

   A B C D E
   47 ☐ ☐ ☐ ☐ ☐

48. <u>The statistics were checked and the report was filed.</u>

   (A) The statistics were checked and the report was filed.
   (B) The statistics and the report were checked and filed.
   (C) The statistics were checked and the report filed.
   (D) The statistics and the report were checked and filed respectively.
   (E) Only after the statistics were checked was the report filed.

   A B C D E
   48 ☐ ☐ ☐ ☐ ☐

49. Dick was awarded a medal for bravery <u>on account he risked his life</u> to save the drowning child.

   (A) on account he risked his life
   (B) being that he risked his life
   (C) when he risked his life
   (D) the reason being on account of his risking his life
   (E) since he had risked his life

   A B C D E
   49 ☐ ☐ ☐ ☐ ☐

50. The teacher asked the newly-admitted student <u>which was the country that she came from.</u>

    (A) which was the country that she came from
    (B) from which country she had come from
    (C) the origin of the country she had come from
    (D) which country have you come from?
    (E) which country she was from

A B C D E
50 ☐ ☐ ☐ ☐ ☐

NOW THAT YOU HAVE COMPLETED PRACTICE TEST 3

1. Turn to the Answer Key on page 56.

2. How many **correct answers** do you have out of 50 questions? ....

3. How many **incorrect answers** do you have out of 50 questions? ....

4. Deduct ¼ of the number of incorrect answers from the number of correct answers to get a **"raw score"** of ....

5. Your **"scaled score"** for this test, according to the Raw Score/Scaled Score Table on page 24 is ....

ANSWER KEY FOR PRACTICE TEST 3

1. E	11. D	21. C	31. A	41. B
2. C	12. D	22. A	32. B	42. A
3. B	13. E	23. B	33. D	43. B
4. B	14. D	24. A	34. E	44. D
5. B	15. C	25. E	35. C	45. E
6. D	16. A	26. B	36. E	46. C
7. E	17. D	27. C	37. B	47. C
8. A	18. A	28. D	38. C	48. A
9. C	19. C	29. C	39. D	49. E
10. C	20. B	30. B	40. E	50. E

EXPLANATORY ANSWERS
FOR PRACTICE TEST 3

1. **(E)** All underlined parts are correct.

2. **(C)** ". . . pulled out his gun *quickly* . . ."
The adverb *quickly*—not the adjective *quick*—should be used to modify the verb *pulled out*.

3. **(B)** ". . . if you *had waited* for an occasion . . ."
In the "if clause" of a past contrary-to-fact condition, one must use the past perfect subjunctive form *had waited*—not the future perfect subjunctive form *would have waited*.

4. **(B)** ". . . *there* is no necessary connection . . ."
We have the expletive use of *there* in this sentence—not the possessive pronoun-adjective *their*.

5. **(B)** ". . . I knew the winner to be *him* . . ."
Since *winner* is the subject of the infinitive *to be*, *winner* is in the objective case. (The subject of an infinitive is always in the objective case.) The predicate noun or pronoun must be in the same case as the subject. Therefore, the predicate pronoun, in this particular case, must have an objective form *(him)*.

6. **(D)** ". . . to express *himself*."
The objective form of the reflexive pronoun is *himself*—not *hisself*.

7. **(E)** All underlined parts are correct.

8. **(A)** "I appreciate *your* helping me . . ."
The subject of a gerund is in the possessive case. We, therefore, say *your helping*—not *you helping*.

9. **(C)** ". . . from the wood, *we* can see the blooming lilac . . ."
The participle *looking* must modify the subject (which comes right after the comma). It is not the *lilac* that is looking—it is *we* or *one*—that is, a person or persons doing the looking.

10. **(C)** "No sooner had he begun to speak *than* . ."
The correct expression is *no sooner . . . than*—not *no sooner . . . when*.

11. **(D)** ". . . raise *their* eyebrows."
The possessive pronoun-adjective is *their*—not *there*.

12. **(D)** ". . . so that he, *not the lady*, would get the cork."
The *lady* is misplaced in the original sentence. As you see, the correct (or incorrect placement) may make quite a difference in the meaning of the sentence.

13. **(E)** All underlined parts are correct.

14. **(D)** ". . . but the field supervisor, the sales manager, and *me*."
The preposition *but* is understood before *me*. Since *me* is the object of the preposition *but*, it has an object form *(me)*—not a nominative form *(I)*.

15. **(C)** ". . . that Williams has an interest *in* and an aptitude for . . ."
The preposition *in* must be included after *interest* in order to introduce the object of the preposition *(chemical experimentation)*

16. **(A)** "Manslaughter *occurs when* a person . . ."
Avoid using *where* to introduce a definition unless the definition pertains to place or location.

17. **(D)** "The reason . . . is *that* they are really insecure."
We say *the reason is that*—not *the reason is because*.

18. **(A)** "*It's* not generally known . . ."
We need here the contraction *It's* (meaning *It is*).

19. **(C)** "... is one of the *most poorly* taught subjects ..."
The participle *taught* must be modified by an adverb (*poorly*—the superlative form of which is *most poorly*)—not by an adjective (*poorest*).

20. **(B)** "Developed by the research engineers of Dupont, the new explosive is considered by the government to be ..."
The participle (*Developed*) is not supposed to modify *the government*—it must modify *the new explosive*. That is the reason we have to rearrange the sentence.

21. **(C)** "From *any one* of them ..."
The word *either* refers to one of two. Since we are dealing here with three things (baseball, football, and soccer), we cannot say *either*.

22. **(A)** "After I *had listened* ..."
We must use the past perfect tense (*had listened*) to indicate an action taking place before another past action (*hurried*).

23. **(B)** "... that the *Mayor's taking* ..."
The possessive form (*Mayor's*) must be used for the noun which modifies the gerund (*taking*).

24. **(A)** "Having set the bag ..."
The verb *to set* means *to place*. The past participle of *to set* is *having set*. The verb *to sit* means *to rest*. The past participle of *to sit* is *having sat*. This sentence requires the use of the transitive verb *to set* — not the intransitive verb *to sit*.

25. **(E)** All underlined parts are correct.

26. **(B)** "... that if Kennedy were alive today ..."
The verb in a condition contrary to fact is *were* for all persons — never *was*.

27. **(C)** "... are strongly opposed to *his* associating with ..."
A pronoun in the possessive case (*his*) — not in the objective case (*him*) — should be used to modify a gerund (*associating*) when that pronoun indicates the person who is performing the action of the gerund.

28. **(D)** "... let *him* speak up."
An indefinite antecedent (*anyone*) must be referred to by a singular pronoun (*him* — not *them*).

29. **(C)** "... to invite my husband, my mother and *me* ..."
All of the words of a compound object must be in the objective case. Note that the words *husband, mother,* and *me* are all direct objects of the infinitive *to invite*.

30. **(B)** "Neither rain nor snow nor sleet *keeps* the postman ..."
When subjects are connected by *neither ... nor*, the verb must agree with the subject which is closest to the verb — *sleet* is the closest subject to the verb (*keeps*) in the sentence. Since *sleet* is singular, the verb (*keeps*) must be singular.

31. **(A)** Choice A is correct. Choice B's passive verb ("was requested") interferes with the flow of the sentence. "It occurred" in Choice C is unnecessary. Choice D is too wordy for what has to be expressed. Choice E changes the meaning of the original sentence — the students did not "insist."

32. **(B)** Choice A is indirect. Choice B is correct. In Choice C, "as a prize" repeats unnecessarily the "Nobel Prize." Choice D is much too awkward. Choice E is incorrect — the scientists did not discover viruses.

33. **(D)** The important thing is not "promptness"; accordingly, Choice A is wrong. Choice B is incorrect because it is not the "loan" that must be returned. In Choice C, "You must understand" is unnecessary. Choice D is correct. Choice E changes the meaning of the original sentence.

34. **(E)** Choice A, as a phrase, hangs without clearly modifying anything else in the sentence. Choice B would be correct if it were preceded and followed by a dash in order to set the choice off from what goes before and after. Choice C is wrong because one does not "amass a scholastic record." Choice D is a complete sentence within a sentence, thus creating a run-on sentence situation. Choice E is correct.

35. **(C)** In Choice A, the use of the passive verb ("were trounced") reduces the effectiveness of expression. Choice B is indirect. Choice C is correct. In Choice D, "which is hard to believe" is unnecessary. Choice E is indirect.

36. **(E)** In Choice A, "are necessary" is not only not necessary, but the expression makes the sentence ungrammatical with the additional complete predicate ("are necessary").
    There are too many "ands" in Choice B. Some grammarians call this an "Andy" sentence.
    In Choice C, "And other fruit... peaches" is an incomplete sentence — also called a sentence fragment. Choice D also suffers from sentence fragmentation: "Such as pineapples and peaches." Choice E is correct.

37. **(B)** In Choice A, it is unidiomatic to say "instruction to learn." Choice B is correct. Choice C is too wordy. Choice D is not as direct as Choice B. Choice E suffers from lack of parallelism.

38. **(C)** Choice A is awkward and wordy. Choice B is indirect. Choice C is correct. Choice D is unacceptable idiomatically even though the meaning intended is there. Choice E changes the meaning of the original sentence.

39. **(D)** Choice A has incorrect punctuation. A dash (not a comma) is required after "that's not all." In Choice B, the expression "another thing" is too general. Choice C changes the meaning of the original sentence. Choice D is correct. Choice E is too indirectly expressed.

40. **(E)** Choice A suffers from too many "ands" (and-itis). Choices B and C are incorrect because they lack parallel construction. In Choice D, the correct form of the infinitive meaning "to rest" is "(to) lie" – not "(to) lay." Choice E is correct.

41. **(B)** Choice A is awkward. Choice B is correct. Choice C is ungrammatical – "courses" cannot act as a direct object after the copulative construction "am not certain." Choice D is too wordy. Choice E does not make sense.

42. **(A)** Choice A is correct. Choice B is too indirectly stated. Choice C is verbose – since the people "had no doubt," there is no need to use the expression "it was clear." Choice D is indirect and awkward. Choice E changes the meaning of the original sentence.

43. **(B)** Choice A is too wordy. Choice B is correct. Choice C is indirectly stated. Choices D and E change the meaning of the original sentence.

44. **(D)** Choice A is indirectly stated. Choice B deviates from the original statement. Choice C makes the whole sentence run-on. Choice D is correct. Choice E changes the meaning of the original sentence.

45. **(E)** Choice A is awkward. Choice B has a meaning which differs from that of the original sentence. Choices C and D are unidiomatic. Choice E is correct.

46. **(C)** Choice A is out-of-date. Choice B does not give the meaning intended in the original sentence. Choice C is correct. Choice D is too wordy. Choice E changes the meaning of the original sentence.

47. **(C)** Choices A, B, D, and E are incorrect because each choice begins its own new sentence. Each of these choices, therefore, creates a run-on sentence. Choice C is correct.

48. **(A)** Choice A is correct. Choices B and E change the meaning of the original sentence. Choice C is incorrect grammatically because the verb ellipsis is im-

proper – "the report *was* filed." Choice D is too involved.

49. **(E)** The expression "on account" in Choice A cannot be used as a subordinate conjunction. The expression "being that" in Choice B is always incorrect. Choice C changes the meaning of the original sentence. Choice D is too wordy. Choice E is correct.

50. **(E)** Choice A is too wordy. The double use of the preposition "from" in Choice B is incorrect. Choice C is too wordy. Choice D, as direct discourse, would be correct with the proper punctuation: ...student, "Which country have you come from?" Choice E is correct.

Practice Test 4 ⟶

USE THIS SHEET FOR YOUR ANSWERS
PRACTICE TEST 4

	A B C D E		A B C D E		A B C D E		A B C D E		A B C D E
1	☐ ☐ ☐ ☐ ☐	11	☐ ☐ ☐ ☐ ☐	21	☐ ☐ ☐ ☐ ☐	31	☐ ☐ ☐ ☐ ☐	41	☐ ☐ ☐ ☐ ☐
2	☐ ☐ ☐ ☐ ☐	12	☐ ☐ ☐ ☐ ☐	22	☐ ☐ ☐ ☐ ☐	32	☐ ☐ ☐ ☐ ☐	42	☐ ☐ ☐ ☐ ☐
3	☐ ☐ ☐ ☐ ☐	13	☐ ☐ ☐ ☐ ☐	23	☐ ☐ ☐ ☐ ☐	33	☐ ☐ ☐ ☐ ☐	43	☐ ☐ ☐ ☐ ☐
4	☐ ☐ ☐ ☐ ☐	14	☐ ☐ ☐ ☐ ☐	24	☐ ☐ ☐ ☐ ☐	34	☐ ☐ ☐ ☐ ☐	44	☐ ☐ ☐ ☐ ☐
5	☐ ☐ ☐ ☐ ☐	15	☐ ☐ ☐ ☐ ☐	25	☐ ☐ ☐ ☐ ☐	35	☐ ☐ ☐ ☐ ☐	45	☐ ☐ ☐ ☐ ☐
6	☐ ☐ ☐ ☐ ☐	16	☐ ☐ ☐ ☐ ☐	26	☐ ☐ ☐ ☐ ☐	36	☐ ☐ ☐ ☐ ☐	46	☐ ☐ ☐ ☐ ☐
7	☐ ☐ ☐ ☐ ☐	17	☐ ☐ ☐ ☐ ☐	27	☐ ☐ ☐ ☐ ☐	37	☐ ☐ ☐ ☐ ☐	47	☐ ☐ ☐ ☐ ☐
8	☐ ☐ ☐ ☐ ☐	18	☐ ☐ ☐ ☐ ☐	28	☐ ☐ ☐ ☐ ☐	38	☐ ☐ ☐ ☐ ☐	48	☐ ☐ ☐ ☐ ☐
9	☐ ☐ ☐ ☐ ☐	19	☐ ☐ ☐ ☐ ☐	29	☐ ☐ ☐ ☐ ☐	39	☐ ☐ ☐ ☐ ☐	49	☐ ☐ ☐ ☐ ☐
10	☐ ☐ ☐ ☐ ☐	20	☐ ☐ ☐ ☐ ☐	30	☐ ☐ ☐ ☐ ☐	40	☐ ☐ ☐ ☐ ☐	50	☐ ☐ ☐ ☐ ☐

Note: At the actual test you will be given an Answer Sheet very much like this sheet in order to record your answers. In doing the following Practice Test, you may prefer to use this Practice Test Answer Sheet. It may, however, be more convenient for you to mark your answer right next to each question. For this method of recording answers, an answer space is, as you will see, provided with each question in this Practice Test.

Standard Written English Practice Test 4

Time: 30 Minutes for the Entire Test

SECTION ONE: GRAMMAR AND USAGE

Directions: In each question, you will find a sentence with four words (or phrases) underlined. In some sentences one of the underlined words (or phrases) is incorrect in the light of the rules of standard written English for grammar, correct usage, and choice of words. No sentence has more than one error. You are to assume that the rest of the sentence (whatever is not underlined) is correct. If you find an error, choose the letter (A *or* B *or* C *or* D) of that underlined word (or phrase) which is incorrect. If you find no error, fill in answer space E.

1. When one <u>leaves</u> his car <u>to be repaired</u>, he <u>assumes</u> that the mechanic
   A   B   C

   will repair the car <u>good</u>. <u>No error.</u>
                        D   E

        A B C D E
   1 ⃝ ⃝ ⃝ ⃝ ⃝

2. Bob could easily <u>have gotten</u> a higher score <u>on</u> his college entrance
                      A   B

   test if he <u>would have read</u> more <u>in his school career.</u> <u>No error.</u>
              C   D   E

        A B C D E
   2 ⃝ ⃝ ⃝ ⃝ ⃝

3. Any <u>modern novelist</u> <u>would be thrilled</u> to have <u>his</u> stories compared
       A   B   C

   <u>with Dickens.</u> <u>No error.</u>
       D   E

        A B C D E
   3 ⃝ ⃝ ⃝ ⃝ ⃝

4. When my <u>Uncle Pancho's</u> plane <u>arrives</u> at the airport <u>in San Diego,</u>
            A   B   C

   I <u>shall already have left</u> San Diego for Mexico City. <u>No error.</u>
      D   E

        A B C D E
   4 ⃝ ⃝ ⃝ ⃝ ⃝

5. Many people in the United States don't scarcely know about the
                                    —A—   —B—
terrible hardships that the Vietnamese are experiencing in their
                                          ————C————
war - ravaged country. No error.
   ——D——   ——E——

A B C D E
5 ☐ ☐ ☐ ☐ ☐

6. Cesar Chavez, president of the United Farm Workers Union,

called for a Congressional investigation of certain California lettuce
—A—

growers whom, he said, were giving bribes to a rival union. No error.
        ——B——   ———C———   ——D——   ——E——

A B C D E
6 ☐ ☐ ☐ ☐ ☐

7. The automobile industry is experimenting with a new type of a motor
                          —————A—————   ———B———
that will consume less gasoline and cause much less pollution. No
                     —C—   ——D——   ——
error.
—E—

A B C D E
7 ☐ ☐ ☐ ☐ ☐

8. The girl who won the beauty contest is nowhere near as beautiful
          ———A———   ————B————
as my mother was when she was a bride. No error.
—C—   —D—   ——E——

A B C D E
8 ☐ ☐ ☐ ☐ ☐

9. Sitting opposite my sister and me in the subway were them same
          ———A———   —B—   ——C——
men who walked alongside us and tried to pinch us on Fifth Avenue.
               ————D————
No error.
——E——

A B C D E
9 ☐ ☐ ☐ ☐ ☐

10. Even if Detroit could provide nonpolluting cars by the original dead-
    ——A——   ————B————
line to meet prescribed Federal standards for clean air, the effect in
             ————C————
big cities would be slight because only new cars would be properly
                                    —D—
equipped. No error.
          ——E——

A B C D E
10 ☐ ☐ ☐ ☐ ☐

11. Of the two.cars that the Smiths have, the Plymouth is,
                             A

    without any question, the cheapest to run. No error.
            B   C   D   E

    11. A B C D E

12. Since one of their members was a prisoner of war in Vietnam, the
            A

    family felt badly when they heard over the radio that the peace talks
            B   C

    were to be discontinued. No error.
         D   E

    12. A B C D E

13. Man cannot live by bread alone, or can he live without bread.
        A   B   C   D

    No error.
    E

    13. A B C D E

14. Have you read in the *Columbia Spectator* that Jeff's leg was broken
          A   B   C

    while playing football? No error.
       D   E

    14. A B C D E

15. Having swam two-thirds of the distance across the English Channel,
       A   B   C

    Dixon could not give up now. No error.
           D   E

    15. A B C D E

16. George Foreman did like he said when he forecast that he would
               A   B

    knock out Joe Frazier to win the world's heavyweight championship.
       C   D

    No error.
    E

    16. A B C D E

17. In the discussion, one speaker held that, since we live in a
                     A

    money-oriented society, the average individual cares little about
         B   C

    solving anyone's else problems. No error.
         D   E

    17. A B C D E

18. Due to the meat boycott, the butchers were doing about half of the
     A   B   C

    business that they were doing previous to the boycott. No error.
              D   E

    18. A B C D E

19. We requested the superintendent of the building to clean up the
    A
    storage room in the basement so that the children had enough space
              B   C   D
    for their bicycles. No error.
                        E

A B C D E
19 ☐ ☐ ☐ ☐ ☐

20. Lidocaine's usefulness as a local anesthetic was discovered by two
    A   B
    Swedish chemists who repeatedly tested the drug's effects on their
                          C   D
    bodies. No error.
            E

A B C D E
20 ☐ ☐ ☐ ☐ ☐

21. Namath played a real fine game in spite of the fact that the Jets
                      A   B
    lost by a touchdown which the opposing team scored in the last
         C   D
    minute of play. No error.
                    E

A B C D E
21 ☐ ☐ ☐ ☐ ☐

22. You may not realize it but the weather in Barbados during Christmas
        A   B   C
    is like New York in June. No error.
       D   E

A B C D E
22 ☐ ☐ ☐ ☐ ☐

23. Stores were jammed with last-minute Christmas shoppers, but the
                A   B
    festive spirit was slightly disrupted by homemade bombs that
                       C
    exploded at two department stores. No error.
    D   E

A B C D E
23 ☐ ☐ ☐ ☐ ☐

24. The teacher did not encourage the student any even though the boy
                                              A
    began to weep when he was told that his poor marks would
          B   C
    likely hold up his graduation. No error.
           D   E

A B C D E
24 ☐ ☐ ☐ ☐ ☐

25. Nixon has stated that he has always had a great interest and ad-
              A   B   C
    miration for the work of the British economist Keynes. No error.
                    D   E

A B C D E
25 ☐ ☐ ☐ ☐ ☐

26. According to the most recent estimates, Greater Miami
        A

has more than 450,000 Spanish-speaking residents, of who
    B   C   D

about 400,000 are Cubans. No error.
                   E

26   A B C D E

27. Sharon planned to pay around a hundred dollars for a new spring
                 A   B

coat but when she saw a gorgeous coat which sold for two hun-
                                 C

dred dollars, she decided to buy it. No error.
              D   E

27   A B C D E

28. Had Lincoln have been alive during World War II, he
           A

would have regarded the racial situation in the armed
       B   C

forces as a throwback to pre-Civil War days. No error.
         D   E

28   A B C D E

29. Members of the staff of the District Attorney made more than
                A

$100,000 from a get-rich-quick scheme in which investors were bilked
             B   C

of about $1-million. No error.
      D   E

29   A B C D E

30. The reason that Roberto Clemente, the great baseball star, was on
        A

the plane that crashed was because he was on his way to help the
           B   C   D

victims of the earthquake. No error.
             E

30   A B C D E

SECTION TWO: SENTENCE CORRECTION

Directions: Each sentence is partly or wholly underlined. In some cases, what is underlined is correct — in
other cases, it is incorrect. The five choices that follow each
sentence represent various ways of writing the underlined
part. Choice A is the same as the original underlining but
Choices B, C, D, and E are different. If, in your judgment,
the original sentence is better than any of the changed sentences, select Choice A. If another choice produces the only
correct sentence, select that other choice (B or C or D or E).

In making your choice, you should observe the rules of
standard written English. Your choice must fulfill the
requirements of correct grammar, diction (word choice),
sentence structure, and punctuation.

If a choice changes the meaning of the original sentence, do not make that choice.

31. At the top of the hill <u>to the left of the tall oak</u> is where they live.

   (A) to the left of the tall oak
   (B) where the tall oak is to the left of it
   (C) and the tall oak is to the left
   (D) left of the tall oak
   (E) to the tall oak's left

31 A B C D E

32. Martin pretended to be asleep <u>whenever she came</u> into the room.

   (A) whenever she came
   (B) at the time she comes
   (C) although she came
   (D) since she came
   (E) by the time she came

31 A B C D E
32 A B C D E

33. Once a person starts taking addictive drugs <u>it is most likely he will
be led to take more.</u>

   (A) it is most likely he will be led to take more
   (B) he will probably take them over and over again
   (C) it is hard to stop him from taking more
   (D) he is likely to continue taking them
   (E) he will have a tendency to continue taking them

33 A B C D E

34. We have not yet been informed concerning the one who broke the window.

    (A) concerning the one who broke the window
    (B) about the identity of the individual who is responsible for breaking the window
    (C) of the window-breaker
    (D) as to who broke the window
    (E) who broke the window

A B C D E
34 ☐ ☐ ☐ ☐ ☐

35. Having the highest marks in his class, the college offered him a scholarship.

    (A) the college offered him a scholarship
    (B) the college offered a scholarship to him
    (C) he was offered a scholarship by the college
    (D) a scholarship was offered him by the college
    (E) a college scholarship was offered to him

A B C D E
35 ☐ ☐ ☐ ☐ ☐

36. The government's failing to keep it's pledges will mean disaster.

    (A) The government's failing to keep it's pledges
    (B) The governments failing to keep it's pledges
    (C) The government's failing to keep its pledges
    (D) The government failing to keep its pledges
    (E) The governments failing to keep their pledges

A B C D E
36 ☐ ☐ ☐ ☐ ☐

37. Her father along with her mother and sister insist that she stop smoking.

    (A) along with her mother and sister insist
    (B) along with her mother and sister insists
    (C) along with her mother and sister are insisting
    (D) along with her mother and sister were insisting
    (E) as well as her mother and sister insist

A B C D E
37 ☐ ☐ ☐ ☐ ☐

38. Most gardeners like to cultivate these kind of flowers in the early spring.

    (A) these kind of flowers
    (B) these kind of flower
    (C) them kinds of flowers
    (D) those kind of flower
    (E) this kind of flowers

A B C D E
38 ☐ ☐ ☐ ☐ ☐

39. The doctor informs us that my aunt has not and never will recover from the fall.

    (A) has not and never will recover
    (B) has not recovered and never will
    (C) has not and never would recover
    (D) has not recovered and never will recover
    (E) had not and never will recover

A B C D E
39 ☐ ☐ ☐ ☐ ☐

40. The senator was neither in favor of <u>or opposed to the proposed leg-</u><u>islation.</u>

    (A) or opposed to the proposed legislation
    (B) and was not opposed to the proposed legislation
    (C) the proposed legislation or opposed to it
    (D) nor opposed to the proposed legislation
    (E) the proposed legislation or opposed to the proposed legislation

    40 A B C D E

41. <u>Glory as well as gain is to be his reward.</u>

    (A) Glory as well as gain is to be his reward.
    (B) As his reward, glory as well as gain is to be his.
    (C) He will be rewarded by glory as well as gain.
    (D) Glory also gain are to be his reward.
    (E) First glory, then gain, will be his reward.

    41 A B C D E

42. She prefers to write poems which describe the slums and <u>study the</u> <u>habits of the underprivileged.</u>

    (A) study the habits of the underprivileged
    (B) study the underprivileged's habits
    (C) studying the habits of the underprivileged
    (D) to study the habits of the underprivileged
    (E) she prefers to study the habits of the underprivileged

    42 A B C D E

43. <u>By studying during weekends, her grades improved surprisingly.</u>

    (A) By studying during weekends, her grades improved surprisingly.
    (B) By studying during weekends, she improved her grades surprisingly.
    (C) She was surprised to find her grades improved after studying during weekends.
    (D) Her grades, by studying during weekends, improved surprisingly.
    (E) Surprisingly, by studying during weekends, her grades improved.

    43 A B C D E

44. The streets here are <u>as dirty as any other city,</u> according to recent research studies.

    (A) as dirty as any other city
    (B) so dirty as any other city
    (C) dirty like any other city
    (D) as dirty as those of any other city
    (E) as those of any city

    44 A B C D E

45. Betty is buxom, <u>with blue eyes, and has a pleasant manner.</u>

    (A) with blue eyes, and has a pleasant manner
    (B) with eyes of blue, and a pleasant manner
    (C) blue-eyed and pleasant
    (D) blue eyes as well as pleasant
    (E) and has blue eyes as well as a pleasant manner

    45 A B C D E

46. If Jack <u>would have listened to his wife</u>, he would not have bought those worthless stocks.

   (A) would have listened to his wife
   (B) would listen to his wife
   (C) had listened to his wife
   (D) listened to what his wife had said
   (E) would have listened to his wife's advice

   A B C D E
   46 ☐ ☐ ☐ ☐ ☐

47. The bank robber approached the teller quietly, cautiously, <u>and in an unpretentious manner.</u>

   (A) and in an unpretentious manner
   (B) and with no pretense
   (C) and by acting unpretentious
   (D) and by acting unpretentiously
   (E) and unpretentiously

   A B C D E
   47 ☐ ☐ ☐ ☐ ☐

48. The conduct of the judge <u>with the accused</u> seemed very unfair to the jury.

   (A) with the accused
   (B) toward the accused
   (C) as to the man who was accused
   (D) and the accused
   (E) as far as the accused was concerned

   A B C D E
   48 ☐ ☐ ☐ ☐ ☐

49. Every typist in the office <u>except she</u> was out sick at least one day during the past month.

   (A) except she   (D) but not her
   (B) except her   (E) outside of her
   (C) excepting she

   A B C D E
   49 ☐ ☐ ☐ ☐ ☐

50. Sam is a professor of theoretical physics, <u>while his brothers are architects</u> with outstanding reputations.

   (A) while his brothers are architects
   (B) also his brothers are architects
   (C) his brothers architects
   (D) as his brothers are architects
   (E) and his brothers are architects

   A B C D E
   50 ☐ ☐ ☐ ☐ ☐

NOW THAT YOU HAVE COMPLETED PRACTICE TEST 4

1. Turn to the Answer Key on page 73.

2. How many **correct answers** do you have out of 50 questions? ....

3. How many **incorrect answers** do you have out of 50 questions? ....

4. Deduct ¼ of the number of incorrect answers from the number of correct answers to get a **"raw score"** of ....

5. Your **"scaled score"** for this test, according to the Raw Score/Scaled Score Table on page 24 is ....

ANSWER KEY FOR PRACTICE TEST 4

1. D	11. C	21. A	31. A	41. A
2. C	12. B	22. D	32. A	42. D
3. D	13. C	23. E	33. D	43. B
4. E	14. D	24. A	34. D	44. D
5. A	15. A	25. C	35. C	45. C
6. B	16. A	26. D	36. C	46. C
7. B	17. D	27. A	37. B	47. E
8. B	18. A	28. A	38. E	48. B
9. C	19. D	29. E	39. D	49. B
10. E	20. E	30. C	40. D	50. E

EXPLANATORY ANSWERS
FOR PRACTICE TEST 4

1. **(D)** "...will repair the car *well*."
The adverb (*well*) — not the adjective (*good*) — is used to modify the verb (*will repair*).

2. **(C)** "...if he *had read* more..."
The "if" clause of a contrary-to-fact past tense requires the verb *had read* — not *would have read*.

3. **(D)** "...to have his stories *compared with those of Dickens*."
We have an improper ellipsis in the original sentence. The additional words (*those of*) are necessary to complete the meaning of the sentence.

4. **(E)** All underlined parts are correct.

5. **(A)** "Many people in the United States *scarcely know*..."
Omit the word *don't*. The word *scarcely* is sufficiently negative to express the meaning intended.

6. **(B)** "...*who*, he said, were giving bribes..."
The subject of the dependent clause must have a nominative case form (*who*) — not an objective case form (*whom*).

7. **(B)** "...with a new *type of* motor..."
Do not use the article *a* or *an* after *kind of, type of, sort of,* etc.

8. **(B)** "...is not *nearly* as beautiful..."
Do not use the expression *nowhere near* for *not nearly*.

9. **(C)** "...were *those* same men..."
The demonstrative pronoun-adjective form (*those*) — not the personal pronoun form (*them*) — must be used to modify the noun *men*.

10. **(E)** All underlined parts are correct.

11. **(C)** "...the *cheaper* to run."
Since we are here comparing two things, we must use the comparative degree — not the superlative degree (*cheapest*).

12. **(B)** "...the family felt *bad*..."
In this sentence, an adjective (*bad*) — not an adverb (*badly*) — is used after a "sense" verb (*felt*).

13. **(C)** "...*nor* can he live without bread."
The coordinate conjunction *nor* is used when the alternative statement is negative.

14. **(D)** "...Jeff's leg was broken while *he was playing* football?"
We have a dangling elliptical clause in the original sentence. We must make clear that *Jeff was playing football*. Otherwise, the sentence may be understood to mean that *Jeff's leg was playing football*.

15. **(A)** "*Having swum* two-thirds of the distance..."
The past participle of *swim* is *having swum*.

16. **(A)** "George Foreman did *as* he said..."
The conjunction (*as*) should be used to introduce the dependent clause (*as he said*) — not the preposition (*like*).

17. **(D)** "...about solving *anyone else's* problems." Say *anyone else's, somebody else's,* etc. Do *not* say *anyone's else, somebody's else.*

18. **(A)** "*Because of* the meat boycott..."
Do not begin a sentence with the words *due to. Due is* an adjective. As an adjective, is must have a noun to modify.

19. **(D)** "...so that the children *would have* enough space..."
In a clause expressing purpose, the subjunctive form of the verb (*would have*) — not the indicative form (*had*) should be used.

20. **(E)** All underlined parts are correct.

21. **(A)** "Namath played a *really* fine game..."
An adverb (*really*) — not an adjective (*real*) — is used to modify the adjective *fine*.

22. **(D)** "... is like *that of* New York in June." We have an improper ellipsis here. We must include the words *that of*, meaning *the weather of*.

23. **(E)** All underlined parts are correct.

24. **(A)** "The teacher did not encourage the student *in any way* even though..."
We cannot properly use the indefinite pronoun *any* to modify the verb (*did not encourage*). The adverbial phrase *in any way* should be used for this purpose.

25. **(C)** "...a great interest *in* and admiration for the work of..."
We are not permitted to omit the preposition *in* since it is necessary to introduce the object of the preposition (*work*).

26. **(D)** "...of *whom* about..."
The object of the preposition must take the objective form (*whom*) — not the nominative form (*who*).

27. **(A)** "Sharon planned to pay *about*..."
About means *approximately;* around means *on all sides*.

28. **(A)** "Had Lincoln *been* alive..."
In a past contrary to fact situation, the "if clause" verb should take the form *had been* — not *had have been*.

29. **(E)** All underlined parts are correct.

30. **(C)** "...was *that* he was on his way..."

31. **(A)** Choice A is correct. Choice B is awkward. The parenthetical effect of Choice C gives the sentence an ungrammatical structure. The ellipsis of "to the" before the beginning of Choice D, is improper. The possessive use ("oak's") in Choice E results in a bad-sounding sentence.

32. **(A)** Choice A is correct. The present tense in Choice B is incorrect. Choices C, D, and E change the meaning of the original sentence.

33. **(D)** Choices A, B, and E are too wordy. Choice C changes the meaning of the original sentence. Choice D is correct.

34. **(D)** Choice A does not come to the point immediately with the use of the expression "concerning the one." Choice B is too wordy. Choice C is not clear. Choice D is correct. Choice E requires an introductory prepositional compound such as "as to."

35. **(C)** Choices A, B, D, and E are incorrect because of a dangling participle error. In these four choices, the participle "Having" must refer to the subject of the sentence. This subject must follow directly after the participial construction ("Having . . . in his class,"). Accordingly, Choice C is the only correct choice.

36. **(C)** Choice A is incorrect because "its" as a possessive pronoun does not take an apostrophe. Choice B is incorrect because the possessive of "government" ("government's") must be used to modify the gerund "failing." Choice C is correct. Choice D is incorrect for the same reason that Choice B is incorrect. Choice E is incorrect for two reasons: (1) it changes the meaning of the original sentence; (2) even if we change the meaning from singularity to plurality, "governments" must correctly be the possessive form "governments'" to modify the gerund "failing."

37. **(B)** The key to getting the correct answer in this question is knowing this grammatical rule: *When explanatory words intervene between the subject and the verb, the number or person of the real subject is not changed.* Note that the subject "father" of the original sentence is singular. Accordingly, Choices A, C, D, and E (each of which has a singular subject, "father") are incorrect with a plural verb. Moreover, Choice D changes the present time of the original sentence to past time. Choice B is correct.

38. **(E)** The demonstrative adjective ("this," "that," "these," "those,") must agree in number with the noun ("kind") it modifies. Accordingly, Choices A, B, and D are incorrect. Choice C is incorrect because the personal pronoun "them" may not be used as an adjective. Choice E is correct.

39. **(D)** Choices A, B, C, and E are incorrect because they suffer from incomplete verb comparision. This is a form of improper ellipsis. The corrections would be as follows: Choice A – "has not recovered"; Choice B – "never will recover"; Choice C – (two corrections necessary) "has not recovered" and "never will recover" (the subjunctive "would" should not be used here). Choice E – "has not recovered." Note that in Choice E, the past perfect tense should not be used. Choice D is correct.

40. **(D)** It is important to know that "neither-nor" go together as correlative conjunctions. The pairing of "neither" with "or" is incorrect. Therefore, Choices A, C and E are incorrect. Choice B is awkward. Choice D is correct.

41. **(A)** Choice A is correct. Note that "Glory" is the singular subject which takes the singular verb "is." "Reward" is the predicate nominative after the copulative verb "is." The other four choices are incorrect because they are indirect and awkward.

42. **(D)** Choices A, B, and C are incorrect because they lack parallelism. Note that the infinitive phrase "to write poems" should balance with the infinitive phrase "to study the habits." Choice D, which does have the parallelism required, is correct. Choice E is too wordy.

43. **(B)** This question is concerned with the correct position of the gerund phrase "By studying." Choice A is incorrect because "grades" have been doing the "studying" with such sentence structure. Choices C, D, and E are incorrect for the same reason. Choice B is correct since "she" is obviously the one who is doing the "studying."

44. **(D)** Choice A is incorrect because of the improper omission of the demonstrative pronoun "those." Choices B and C are incorrect for the same reason. Choice D is correct. Choice E is incorrect because we must bring out the comparison with *another* city.

45. **(C)** Parallelism is the important consideration here. Choice C is correct as the only choice that fulfills the requirements of parallel structure.

46. **(C)** Sequence of tenses in contrary-to-fact past situations requires the "had listened" form of the verb. Choice C is therefore correct and all the other choices are incorrect. Moreover, in Choice E, there is no need to use the word "advice" since the rest of the choice implies that advice has been given.

47. **(E)** Choice E is the only correct choice since the other choices lack parallelism. Choice D is incorrect for an additional reason – the predicate adjective "unpretentious" not the adverb "unpretentiously") should be used after the copulative verbal "acting".

48. **(B)** Choice A is incorrect because it is unidiomatic. Choice B is correct. Choices C and E are incorrect because they are too wordy. Choice D improperly omits "conduct of the (accused)."

49. **(B)** The object form of the pronoun must be used for the object of any preposition. Therefore, Choices A and C are incorrect and Choice B is correct. Choice D is incorrect because we need the nominative form of the personal pronoun ("she") as the subject ("but not she"). Choice E is incorrect because it is too informal for the context.

50. **(E)** Choice A is incorrect because "while" pertains to time and should not be substituted loosely for "and." Choice B is incorrect because it does not tie up grammatically with the rest of the sentence. Choice C is incorrect for the same reason. Choice D is incorrect because the subordinate conjunction "as" does not make sense here. Choice E is correct.

Practice Test 5 ⟶

USE THIS SHEET FOR YOUR ANSWERS
PRACTICE TEST 5

	A B C D E		A B C D E		A B C D E		A B C D E		A B C D E
1	0 0 0 0 0	11	0 0 0 0 0	21	0 0 0 0 0	31	0 0 0 0 0	41	0 0 0 0 0
2	0 0 0 0 0	12	0 0 0 0 0	22	0 0 0 0 0	32	0 0 0 0 0	42	0 0 0 0 0
3	0 0 0 0 0	13	0 0 0 0 0	23	0 0 0 0 0	33	0 0 0 0 0	43	0 0 0 0 0
4	0 0 0 0 0	14	0 0 0 0 0	24	0 0 0 0 0	34	0 0 0 0 0	44	0 0 0 0 0
5	0 0 0 0 0	15	0 0 0 0 0	25	0 0 0 0 0	35	0 0 0 0 0	45	0 0 0 0 0
6	0 0 0 0 0	16	0 0 0 0 0	26	0 0 0 0 0	36	0 0 0 0 0	46	0 0 0 0 0
7	0 0 0 0 0	17	0 0 0 0 0	27	0 0 0 0 0	37	0 0 0 0 0	47	0 0 0 0 0
8	0 0 0 0 0	18	0 0 0 0 0	28	0 0 0 0 0	38	0 0 0 0 0	48	0 0 0 0 0
9	0 0 0 0 0	19	0 0 0 0 0	29	0 0 0 0 0	39	0 0 0 0 0	49	0 0 0 0 0
10	0 0 0 0 0	20	0 0 0 0 0	30	0 0 0 0 0	40	0 0 0 0 0	50	0 0 0 0 0

Note: At the actual test you will be given an Answer Sheet very much like this sheet in order to record your answers. In doing the following Practice Test, you may prefer to use this Practice Test Answer Sheet. It may, however, be more convenient for you to mark your answer right next to each question. For this method of recording answers, an answer space is, as you will see, provided with each question in this Practice Test.

Standard Written English
Practice Test 5

Time: 30 Minutes for the Entire Test

SECTION ONE: GRAMMAR AND USAGE

Directions: In each question, you will find a sentence with four words (or phrases) underlined. In some sentences one of the underlined words (or phrases) is incorrect in the light of the rules of standard written English for grammar, correct usage, and choice of words. No sentence has more than one error. You are to assume that the rest of the sentence (whatever is not underlined) is correct. If you find an error, choose the letter (A *or* B *or* C *or* D) of that underlined word (or phrase) which is incorrect. If you find no error, fill in answer space E.

1. Besides being an outstanding student, he is also a leader in school
   A   B   C
   government and a trophy-winner in school sports. No error.
                    D   E

   A B C D E
   1 ▯ ▯ ▯ ▯ ▯

2. If any signer of the Constitution was to return to life for a day, his
                                     A   B
   opinion of our amendments would be interesting. No error.
              C   D   E

   A B C D E
   2 ▯ ▯ ▯ ▯ ▯

3. The dean of the college, together with some other faculty members,
              A   B
   are planning a conference for the purpose of laying down certain
   C   D
   regulations. No error.
                E

   A B C D E
   3 ▯ ▯ ▯ ▯ ▯

4. If one lives in Florida one day and in Iceland the next, he is certain to
                    A   B   C   D
   feel the change in temperature. No error.
                                   E

   A B C D E
   4 ▯ ▯ ▯ ▯ ▯

5. <u>Now</u> that the stress of examinations and interviews <u>are</u> over, we can
   A B

   all <u>relax</u> for <u>awhile</u>. <u>No error</u>.
   C D E

A B C D E
5 ▢ ▢ ▢ ▢ ▢

6. The industrial <u>trend</u> <u>is</u> in the direction of <u>more</u> machines and <u>less</u>
   A B C D

   people. <u>No error</u>.
   E

A B C D E
6 ▢ ▢ ▢ ▢ ▢

7. The American standard of living is still <u>higher</u> <u>than</u> <u>most of the</u>
   A B C

   <u>other countries of the world.</u> <u>No error</u>.
   D E

A B C D E
7 ▢ ▢ ▢ ▢ ▢

8. <u>At last,</u> <u>late</u> in the afternoon, a long line of flags and colored umbrellas
   A B

   <u>were</u> seen moving <u>toward</u> the gate of the palace. <u>No error</u>.
   C D E

A B C D E
8 ▢ ▢ ▢ ▢ ▢

9. <u>Due to</u> the failure of the air-cooling system, many in the audience
   A

   <u>had left</u> the meeting <u>before</u> the principal speaker <u>arrived</u>. <u>No error</u>.
   B C D E

A B C D E
9 ▢ ▢ ▢ ▢ ▢

10. Psychologists and psychiatrists <u>will tell</u> us that it is of utmost impor-
    A

    tance that a <u>disturbed</u> child <u>receive</u> professional attention <u>as soon as</u>
    B C D

    possible. <u>No error</u>.
    E

A B C D E
10 ▢ ▢ ▢ ▢ ▢

11. <u>After waiting in line</u> for three hours, <u>much to our disgust,</u> the tickets
    A B C

    <u>had been</u> sold out when we reached the window. <u>No error</u>.
    D E

A B C D E
11 ▢ ▢ ▢ ▢ ▢

12. That angry outburst of <u>Father's</u> last night was so annoying that it
    A

    resulted in our <u>guests</u> <u>packing up</u> and leaving <u>this</u> morning. <u>No error</u>.
    B C D E

A B C D E
12 ▢ ▢ ▢ ▢ ▢

13. Sharp advances last week in the wholesale price of beef is a strong
    ____A____   ____B____
    indication of higher meat costs to come, but so far retail prices con-
                            __C__
    tine favorable. No error.
         __D__   ___E___
                                                 A B C D E
                                              13 ⃞ ⃞ ⃞ ⃞ ⃞

14. An acquaintance with the memoirs of Elizabeth Barrett Browning
    and Robert Browning enable us to appreciate the depth of influence
                         ___A___   _____B_____
    that two people of talent can have on each other. No error.
                                      __C__ ____D____ ___E___
                                                 A B C D E
                                              14 ⃞ ⃞ ⃞ ⃞ ⃞

15. The supervisor was advised to give the assignment to whomever
                     ___A___   ____B____
    he believed had a strong sense of responsibility, and the courage of his
    __C__   __D__
    conviction. No error.
              ___E___
                                                 A B C D E
                                              15 ⃞ ⃞ ⃞ ⃞ ⃞

16. If he would have lain quietly as instructed by the doctor, he might not
       ____A____ __B__   _____C_____
    have had a second heart attack. No error.
    __D__   ___E___
                                                 A B C D E
                                              16 ⃞ ⃞ ⃞ ⃞ ⃞

17. The founder and, for many years, the guiding spirit of the "Kenyon
                    _____A_____   _____B_____
    Review" is John Crowe Ransom, who you must know as an out-
                                 __C__   __D__
    standing American critic. No error.
                            ___E___
                                                 A B C D E
                                              17 ⃞ ⃞ ⃞ ⃞ ⃞

18. Though you may not agree with the philosophy of Malcolm X, you
    ___A___   ____B____
    must admit that he had tremendous influence over a great many
                      __C__   __D__
    followers. No error.
             ___E___
                                                 A B C D E
                                              18 ⃞ ⃞ ⃞ ⃞ ⃞

19. There is no objection to <u>him</u> joining the party <u>provided</u> he is willing
A   B

to <u>fit in with</u> the plans of the group and is <u>ready and able</u> to do his
C   D

share of the work. <u>No error.</u>
E

A B C D E
19 ☐ ☐ ☐ ☐ ☐

20. <u>Ceremonies</u> <u>were opened</u> by a drum and bugle corps of Chinese chil-
A   B

dren <u>parading up</u> Mott Street in <u>colorful uniforms.</u> <u>No error.</u>
C   D   E

A B C D E
20 ☐ ☐ ☐ ☐ ☐

21. The reason <u>most</u> Americans <u>don't</u> pay much attention to <u>rising</u> African
A   B   C

nationalism is <u>because</u> they really do not know modern Africa.
D

<u>No error.</u>
E

A B C D E
21 ☐ ☐ ☐ ☐ ☐

22. The farmer felt <u>badly</u> about his prize <u>cow's</u> being <u>eliminated</u> from
A   B   C

<u>competition.</u> <u>No error.</u>
D   E

A B C D E
22 ☐ ☐ ☐ ☐ ☐

23. The Federal Aviation Administration <u>ordered</u> an emergency inspec-
A

tion <u>of several</u> Pan American planes <u>on account of</u> a Pan American
B   C

Boeing 707 <u>had crashed</u> on Bali, in Indonesia. <u>No error.</u>
D   E

A B C D E
23 ☐ ☐ ☐ ☐ ☐

24. A gang <u>of armed thieves,</u> directed by a young woman, <u>has raided</u> the
A   B

mansion of a <u>gold-mining</u> millonaire <u>near Dublin</u> late last night.
C   D

<u>No error.</u>
E

A B C D E
24 ☐ ☐ ☐ ☐ ☐

25. I had a male <u>chauvinist pig</u> dream that the women of the world <u>rose up</u>
A   B   C

and denounced the <u>women's</u> liberation movement. <u>No error.</u>
D   E

A B C D E
25 ☐ ☐ ☐ ☐ ☐

26. On April 8, 1974, Henry Aaron hit his 715th home run, and breaking
    <u>A</u>   <u>B</u>   <u>C</u>

    Babe <u>Ruth's</u> record. <u>No error.</u>
        D   E

                                               A B C D E
                                         26 ▯ ▯ ▯ ▯ ▯

27. Since their attempt <u>at a reconciliation</u> <u>has ended</u> <u>in failure,</u> Elizabeth
                          A   B   C

    Taylor and Richard Burton will file <u>for divorcing.</u> <u>No error.</u>
                                  D   E

                                                 A B C D E
                                         27 ▯ ▯ ▯ ▯ ▯

28. The long <u>lines of cars</u> at gasoline stations have disappeared <u>like as if</u>
               A   B

    there <u>were</u> never an <u>energy crisis.</u> <u>No error.</u>
          C   D   E

                                               A B C D E
                                         28 ▯ ▯ ▯ ▯ ▯

29. The residents of the town of Hillsborough, where Patricia <u>Hearst's</u>
                                                      A

    parents <u>live,</u> <u>is getting</u> lessons <u>on how</u> to protect themselves from
            B   C   D

    kidnapping. <u>No error.</u>
               E

                                               A B C D E
                                         29 ▯ ▯ ▯ ▯ ▯

30. The man told <u>his son</u> <u>to take</u> the car to the <u>service</u> station because
                   A   B   C

    it needed gasoline. <u>No error.</u>
    <u>D</u>   E

                                               A B C D E
                                         30 ▯ ▯ ▯ ▯ ▯

SECTION TWO: SENTENCE CORRECTION

Directions: Each sentence is partly or wholly underlined. In some cases, what is underlined is correct — in other cases, it is incorrect. The five choices that follow each sentence represent various ways of writing the underlined part. Choice A is the same as the original underlining but Choices B, C, D, and E are different. If, in your judgment, the original sentence is better than any of the changed sentences, select Choice A. If another choice produces the only correct sentence, select that other choice (B or C or D or E).

In making your choice, you should observe the rules of standard written English. Your choice must fulfill the requirements of correct grammar, diction (word choice), sentence structure, and punctuation.

If a choice changes the meaning of the original sentence, do not make that choice.

31. <u>Such of his novels as was humorous were successful.</u>

   (A) Such of his novels as was humorous were successful.
   (B) Such of his novels as were humorous were successful.
   (C) His novels such as were humorous were successful.
   (D) His novels were successful and humorous.
   (E) Novels such as his humorous ones were sucessful.

                                                  A B C D E
                                              31 0 0 0 0 0

32. <u>Being that the plane was grounded, we stayed over</u> till the next morning so that we could get the first flight out.

   (A) Being that the plane was grounded, we stayed over
   (B) In view of the fact that the plane was grounded, we stayed over
   (C) Since the plane was grounded, we stayed over
   (D) Because the plane was grounded, we stood over
   (E) On account of the plane being grounded, we stayed over

                                                A B C D E
                                              32 0 0 0 0 0

33. <u>He never has and he never will</u> keep his word.

   (A) He never has and he never will
   (B) He has never yet and never will
   (C) He has not ever and he will not
   (D) He never has or will
   (E) He never has kept and he never will

                                                A B C D E
                                              33 0 0 0 0 0

34. The teacher felt badly because she had scolded the bright child who was restless for want of something to do.

    (A) felt badly because she had scolded the bright child
    (B) felt badly why she had scolded the bright child
    (C) felt bad because she had scolded the bright child
    (D) felt bad by scolding the bright child
    (E) had felt badly because she scolded the bright child

    34 A B C D E
       □ □ □ □ □

35. This book does not describe the struggle of the Blacks to win their voting rights that I bought.

    (A) does not describe the struggle of the Blacks to win their voting rights that I bought
    (B) does not describe the Black struggle to win their voting rights that I bought
    (C) does not, although I bought it, describe the struggle of the Blacks to win their voting rights
    (D) which I bought does not describe the struggle to win for Blacks their voting rights
    (E) that I bought does not describe the struggle of the Blacks to win their voting rights

    35 A B C D E
       □ □ □ □ □

36. Barbara cannot help but think that she will win a college scholarship.

    (A) Barbara cannot help but think
    (B) Barbara cannot help but to think
    (C) Barbara cannot help not to think
    (D) Barbara can help but think
    (E) Barbara cannot but help thinking

    36 A B C D E
       □ □ □ □ □

37. In spite of Tom wanting to study, his sister made him wash the dishes.

    (A) Tom wanting to study
    (B) the fact that Tom wanted to study
    (C) Tom's need to study
    (D) Tom's wanting to study
    (E) Tom studying

    37 A B C D E
       □ □ □ □ □

38. The old sea captain told my wife and me many interesting yarns about his many voyages.

    (A) my wife and me
    (B) me and my wife
    (C) my wife and I
    (D) I and my wife
    (E) my wife along with me

    38 A B C D E
       □ □ □ □ □

39. A great many students from several universities <u>are planning to, if the weather is favorable,</u> attend next Saturday's mass rally in Washington.

   (A) are planning to, if the weather is favorable, attend next Saturday's mass rally in Washington

   (B) are planning, if the weather is favorable, to attend next Saturday's mass rally in Washington

   (C) are planning to attend, if the weather is favorable, next Saturday's mass rally in Washington

   (D) are planning to attend next Saturday's mass rally in Washington, if the weather is favorable

   (E) are, if the weather is favorable, planning to attend next Saturday's mass rally in Washington

                                      A B C D E
                                    39 ☐ ☐ ☐ ☐ ☐

40. Jane's body movements are <u>like those of a dancer.</u>

   (A) like those of a dancer

   (B) the same as a dancer

   (C) like a dancer

   (D) a dancer's

   (E) like those of a dancer's

                                        A B C D E
                                    40 ☐ ☐ ☐ ☐ ☐

41. This is one restaurant I won't patronize because <u>I was served a fried egg by the waitress that was rotten.</u>

   (A) I was served a fried egg by the waitress that was rotten

   (B) I was served by the waitress a fried egg that was rotten

   (C) a fried egg was served to me by the waitress that was rotten

   (D) the waitress served me a fried egg that was rotten

   (E) a rotten fried egg was served to me by the waitress

                                        A B C D E
                                    41 ☐ ☐ ☐ ☐ ☐

42. Watching the familiar story unfold on the screen, he was glad <u>that he read the book with such painstaking attention to detail.</u>

   (A) that he read the book with such painstaking attention to detail.

   (B) that he had read the book with such painstaking attention to detail.

   (C) that he read the book with such attention to particulars.

   (D) that he read the book with such intense effort.

   (E) that he paid so much attention to the plot of the book.

                                        A B C D E
                                    42 ☐ ☐ ☐ ☐ ☐

43. If anyone requested tea instead of coffee, <u>it was a simple matter to serve it to them</u> from the large percolator at the rear of the table.

   (A) it was a simple matter to serve it to them

   (B) it was easy to serve them

   (C) it was a simple matter to serve them

   (D) it was a simple matter to serve it to him

   (E) he could serve himself

                                        A B C D E
                                    43 ☐ ☐ ☐ ☐ ☐

44. He bought <u>some bread, butter, cheese and decided</u> not to eat them until the evening.

    (A) some bread, butter, cheese and decided
    (B) some bread, butter, cheese and then decided
    (C) a little bread, butter, cheese and decided
    (D) some bread, butter, cheese, deciding
    (E) some bread, butter, and cheese and decided

    A B C D E
    44 ▯ ▯ ▯ ▯ ▯

45. The things the children liked best were <u>swimming in the river and to watch the horses being groomed by the trainer.</u>

    (A) swimming in the river and to watch the horses being groomed by the trainer.
    (B) swimming in the river and to watch the trainer grooming the horses.
    (C) that they liked to swim in the river and watch the horses being groomed by the trainer.
    (D) swimming in the river and watching the horses being groomed by the trainer.
    (E) to swimming the river and watching the horses being groomed by the trainer.

    A B C D E
    45 ▯ ▯ ▯ ▯ ▯

46. A reward was offered <u>to whoever would return the dog to its owner.</u>

    (A) to whoever would return the dog to its owner.
    (B) to whomever would return the dog to its owner.
    (C) to whosoever would return the dog to its owner.
    (D) to whomsoever would return the dog to its owner.
    (E) to whichever person would return the dog to its owner.

    A B C D E
    46 ▯ ▯ ▯ ▯ ▯

47. <u>Irregardless of the outcome of the battle,</u> neither side will be able to claim a decisive victory.

    (A) Irregardless of the outcome of the battle,
    (B) Irregardless of how the battle ends,
    (C) Regardless of the outcome of the battle,
    (D) Despite the outcome of the battle,
    (E) Irregardless of the battle,

    A B C D E
    47 ▯ ▯ ▯ ▯ ▯

48. One of the finest examples of early Greek sculpture <u>are to be found in the British Museum</u> in London.

    (A) are to be found in the British Museum
    (B) were to be found in the British Museum
    (C) are found in the British Museum
    (D) is to be found in the British Museum
    (E) are in the British Museum

    A B C D E
    48 ▯ ▯ ▯ ▯ ▯

49. We were surprised at him canceling the order without giving any previous indication of his intentions.

(A) We were surprised at him canceling the order without giving any previous indication of his intentions.

(B) We were surprised that he canceled the order and didn't tell anyone.

(C) His canceling the order surprised us all.

(D) We were surprised at his canceling the order without giving any previous indication of his intentions.

(E) We were surprised at him canceling the order and not letting anyone know about it.

49 A B C D E 〇〇〇〇〇

50. When going for an interview, a high school graduate should be prepared to answer the questions that will be asked of him without hesitation.

(A) a high school graduate should be prepared to answer the questions that will be asked of him without hesitation.

(B) a high school graduate should without hesitation be prepared to answer the questions that will be asked of him.

(C) a high school graduate should be prepared without hesitation to answer the questions that will be asked of him.

(D) a high school graduate should be prepared to answer without hesitation the questions that will be asked of him.

(E) a high school graduate should be prepared to answer the questions without hesitation that will be asked of him.

50 A B C D E 〇〇〇〇〇

NOW THAT YOU HAVE COMPLETED PRACTICE TEST 5

1. Turn to the Answer Key on page 92.

2. How many **correct answers** do you have out of 50 questions? ....

3. How many **incorrect answers** do you have out of 50 questions? ....

4. Deduct ¼ of the number of incorrect answers from the number of correct answers to get a **"raw score"** of ....

5. Your **"scaled score"** for this test, according to the Raw Score/Scaled Score Table on page 24 is ....

ANSWER KEY FOR PRACTICE TEST 5

1. E	11. C	21. D	31. B	41. D
2. A	12. B	22. A	32. C	42. B
3. C	13. B	23. C	33. E	43. D
4. E	14. A	24. B	34. C	44. E
5. B	15. B	25. E	35. E	45. D
6. D	16. A	26. C	36. A	46. A
7. C	17. C	27. D	37. D	47. C
8. C	18. E	28. B	38. A	48. D
9. A	19. A	29. C	39. D	49. D
10. E	20. D	30. D	40. A	50. D

EXPLANATORY ANSWERS
FOR PRACTICE TEST 5

1. **(E)** All underlined parts are correct.

2. **(A)** "If any signer of the Constitution *were* to return to life . . ."
The verb in the "if clause" of a present contrary-to-fact conditional statement must have a past subjunctive form *(were)*.

3. **(C)** "The dean of the college . . . *is* planning . . ."
The subject of the sentence *(dean)* is singular. Therefore, the verb must be singular *(is planning)*.

4. **(E)** All underlined parts are correct.

5. **(B)** "Now that the stress . . . *is* over . . ."
The subject of the subordinate clause is singular *(stress)*. Accordingly, the verb of the clause must be singular *(is*—not *are)*. Incidentally, *examinations* and *interviews* are not subjects—they are objects of the preposition *of*.

6. **(D)** ". . . of more machines and *fewer* people."
We use *fewer* for persons and things that may be counted. We use *less* for bulk or mass.

7. **(C)** ". . . than *that of most* of the other countries of the world."
We must have paralellism so that the word *standard* in the main clause of the sentence acts as an antecedent for the pronoun *that* in the subordinate clause. As the original sentence reads, the American standard of living is still higher than the countries themselves.

8. **(C)** ". . . a long line of flags . . . *was seen* . . ."
The subject of the sentence is singular *(line)*. Therefore, the verb must be singular *(was seen)*.

9. **(A)** "*Because of* the failure . . ."
Never start a sentence with *Due to*.

10. **(E)** All underlined parts are correct.

11. **(C)** "After waiting in line for three hours, the tickets had, *much to our disgust*, been sold out when we reached the window."
Avoid squinting constructions—that is, modifiers that are so placed that the reader cannot tell whether they are modifying the words immediately preceding the construction, or the words immediately following the construction.

12. **(B)** ". . . resulted in our *guests'* packing up . . ."
A noun or pronoun immediately preceding a gerund is in the possessive case. Note that the noun *guests* followed by an apostrophe is possessive.

13. **(B)** "Sharp advances . . . *are* . . ."
Since the subject of the sentence is plural *(advances)*, the verb must be plural *(are)*.

14. **(A)** "An acquaintance with the memoirs . . . *enables* us . . ."
Since the subject of the sentence is singular *(acquaintance)*, the verb must be singular *(enables)*.

15. **(B)** ". . . to *whoever* . . . had a strong sense . . ."
The subject of the subordinate clause is *whoever* and it takes a nominative form *(whoever*—not *whomever)* since it is a subject. Incidentally, the expression *he believed* is parenthetical so that it has no grammatical relationship with the rest of the sentence.

16. **(A)** "If he *had lain* . . ."
The verb in the "if clause" of a past contrary-to-fact conditional statement must take the *had lain* form—not the *would have lain* form.

17. **(C)** ". . . John Crowe Ransom, *whom* you must know as an outstanding American critic."
The direct object of the subordinate clause—or of any clause or sentence—must be in the objective case and, accordingly, must take the objective form (*whom*—not *who*).

18. **(E)** All underlined parts are correct.

19. **(A)** "There is no objection to *his* joining . . .
We have here a pronoun that is acting as the subject of the gerund *joining*. As a subject of the gerund, the pronoun must be in the possessive case (*his*).

20. **(D)** ". . . of Chinese children parading *in colorful uniforms* up Mott Street."
In the original sentence, *in colorful uniforms* was a misplaced modifier.

21. **(D)** "The reason . . . is *that* . . ."
We must say *the reason is that*—not *the reason is because.*

22. **(A)** "The farmer felt *bad* about . . ."
After the copulative verb *(felt)*, the word referring to the subject is a predicate adjective *(bad)*—not an adverb *(badly).*

23. **(C)** ". . . *because* a Pan American Boeing 707 had crashed . . ."
The word group *on account of* has the function of a preposition. We need a subordinate conjunction *(because)* here in order to introduce the clause.

24. **(B)** ". . . *raided* the mansion . . ."
The past tense *(raided)* — not the present perfect tense *(has raided)* — is necessary because the sentence has a specific past time reference *(last night).*

25. **(E)** All underlined parts are correct.

26. **(C)** ". . . *breaking* Babe Ruth's record."
The unnecessary conjunction *and* makes the sentence awkward.

27. **(D)** " . . . will file *for divorce.*"
The idiom is "to file for divorce" — not "to file for divorcing."

28. **(B)** " . . . disappeared *as if* . . . "
The correct expression is "as if" — not "like as if." Incidentally, Choice C *(were)* is correct because it is the correct form of the contrary-to-fact conditional.

29. **(C)** " . . . *are* getting lessons . . . "
The subject *(residents)* is plural. Therefore the verb *(are getting)* must be plural.

30. **(D)** ". . . because *the car* needed gasoline.
The pronoun *it* has an indefinite antecedent. We cannot tell whether *it* refers to the car or the service station. Accordingly, we must be specific by using *car* instead of *it.*

31. **(B)** Choice A is incorrect because the plural verb ("were") is necessary. The reason for the plural verb is that the subject "as" acts as a relative pronoun whose antecedent is the plural noun "novels." Choice B is correct. Choice C is awkward. Choice D changes the meaning of the original sentence – so does Choice E.

32. **(C)** Choice A is incorrect – never start a sentence with "being that." Choice B is too wordy. Choice C is correct. Choice D is incorrect because we "stayed" – not "stood." Choice E is incorrect because "on account of" may never be used as a subordinate conjunction.

33. **(E)** Avoid improper ellipsis. Choices A, B, C, and D are incorrect for this reason. Choice E is correct. The word "kept" must be included since the second part of the sentence uses another form of the verb ("keep").

34. **(C)** Choice A is incorrect because the copulative verb "felt" takes a predicate adjective ("bad") — not an adverb ("badly"). Choice B is incorrect for the same reason. Moreover, we don't say "felt bad why." Choice C is correct. Choice D is incorrect because the verbal phrase "by scolding" is awkward in this context. Choice E is incorrect because of the use of "badly" and because the past

perfect form of the verb ("had felt") is wrong in this time sequence.

35. **(E)** Choices A, B, and C are incorrect because the part of the sentence that deals with the buying of the book is in the wrong position. Choice D is incorrect because the meaning of the original sentence has been changed. According to this' choice, others besides Blacks have been struggling. Choice E is correct.

36. **(A)** Choice A is correct. The other choices are unidiomatic.

37. **(D)** Choice A is incorrect because the possessive form of the noun ("Tom's") must be used to modify the gerund ("wanting"). Choice B is too wordy. Choice C changes the meaning of the original sentence. Choice D is correct. Choice E is incorrect for the same reason that Choice A is incorrect. Also, Choice E changes the meaning of the original sentence.

38. **(A)** Choice A is correct. Choice B is incorrect because "wife" should precede "me." Choice C is incorrect because the object form "me" (not the nominative form "I") should be used as the indirect object. Choice D is incorrect for the reasons given above for Choices B and C. Choice E is too roundabout.

39. **(D)** Choices A, B, C, and E are incorrect because of the misplacement of the sub-ordinate clause ("if the weather is fa-vorable"). Choice D is correct.

40. **(A)** Choices B and C are incorrect because of improper ellipsis. The words "those of" are necessary in these choices. Choice D is incorrect because the "body movements" are not "a dancer's." The possessive use of "dancer's" is incorrect in Choice E.

41. **(D)** The clause "that was rotten" is mis-placed in Choices A, B, and C. Choice D is correct. Choice E is incorrect because the passive use of the verb is not as ef-fective as the active use, in this context.

42. **(B)** Choice A uses wrong tense sequence. Since the reading of the book took place before the watching of the picture, the reading should be expressed in the past perfect tense, which shows action prior to the simple past tense. Choice B cor-rects the error with the use of the past perfect tense, "had read," instead of the past tense, "read." Choices C, D, and E do not correct the mistake, and Choice E in addition changes the meaning.

43. **(D)** Choices A is wrong because the word "them," being plural, cannot properly take the singular antecedent, "anyone." Choices B and C do not correct this error. Choice D corrects it by substituting "him" for "them." Choice E, while correcting the error, changes the meaning of the sentence.

44. **(E)** Choice A contains a "false series," meaning that the word "and" connects the three words in the series — bread, but-ter, cheese — with a wholly different clause, instead of with a similar fourth word. The series, therefore, needs its own "and" to complete it. Only Choice E furnishes this additional "and."

45. **(D)** Choice A violates the principle of parallel structure. If the first thing the children liked was "swimming" (a ger-und), then the second thing they liked should be, not "to watch" (an infinitive), but "watching" (the gerund). Choice B does not improve the sentence. Choice C repeats the beginning of the sentence with the repetitious words "that they liked." Choice D is correct. Choice E simply re-verses the gerund and the infinitive with-out correcting the error.

46. **(A)** Choice A is correct. Choice B wrongly substitutes the objective case "whom-ever" for the nominative "whoever," the subject of the verb "would return." Choice C uses the the form "whosoever," which while correct, is legalistic and not needed here. Choice D again uses the objective case. Choice E is awkward.

47. **(C)** There is no such word as "irregard-less." Therefore Choices A, B, and E

cannot be right. "Despite" in Choice D does not give the same meaning as "regardless." Choice C is the correct one.

48. **(D)** Choice A wrongly uses the plural verb "are to be found" after the subject of the sentence, "One." (The plural word "examples" is not the subject of the prepositional phrase "of the finest examples.") Choice B simply uses the same plural verb in the past tense instead of the present. Choice C does not correct the error. Choice D does, by using the singular verb "is." Choice E is incorrect because of the use of the plural verb "are."

49. **(D)** Choice A fails to use the possessive case of the pronoun that governs a gerund. Choice B changes the meaning of the sentence. Choice C corrects the error but omits a necessary part of the meaning. Choice D is correct. Choice E retains the error of Choice A and, in addition, distorts the meaning of the sentence.

50. **(D)** Choices A, B, C, and E should place the adverbial phrase "without hesitation" after the infinitive it modifies, "to answer." Since the meaning is to "answer without hesitation," the phrase "without hesitation" should be placed right after the infinitive "to answer." This is done in Choice D.

Part Two

·

Grammar and Usage Refresher

The following pages will prove very helpful since you will find in these pages a brief but to-the-point review for every type of question which appears in the actual Standard Written English test.

This "Refresher" includes the following essential areas of Grammar and Usage:

The Parts of Speech	**Tense**
Clauses and Phrases	**Verbals**
The Sentence and Its Parts	**Mood and Voice**
Verbs	**Adjective Modifiers**
Nouns and Pronouns	**Adverbial Modifiers**
Subject-Verb Relationship	**Connectives**

Correct Usage: Choosing the Right Word

GRAMMAR AND USAGE REFRESHER*

CHAPTER 1
The Parts of Speech

1a   Noun

A **noun** is a word that names a **person, place, thing** or **idea.**

Persons	Places	Things	Ideas
nurse	forest	banana	love
Henry	Miami	shoe	democracy
uncle	house	television	hunger
Chicano	airport	notebook	cooperation

A noun that is made up of more than one word is called a **compound noun.**

Persons	Places	Things	Ideas
Martin Luther King	high school	telephone book	energy crisis
cab driver	Puerto Rico	car key	arms race
movie star	dining room	park bench	light year
federal judge	Middle East	pork chop	market value

1b   Pronoun

A **pronoun** is a word used **in place of a noun.**

> Buy a newspaper and bring **it** home.
>   (The pronoun "it" stands for the noun "newspaper.")

> Marlene went to the party but **she** didn't stay long.
>   (The "pronoun "she" stands for the noun "Marlene.")

A **pronoun** may be used **in place of a noun or a group of nouns.**

> Pedro wanted to see the polar bears, camels, and tropical birds, **which** were at the zoo.
>   (The pronoun "which" stands for the nouns "polar bears, camels, and tropical birds.")

> When Mark, Steven, Teresa, and Barbara became eighteen, **they** registered to vote.
>   (The pronoun "they" stands for the nouns "Mark, Steven, Teresa and Barbara.")

The **noun that the pronoun replaces** is called the **antecedent** of the pronoun.

> The **plates** broke when **they** fell.
>   (The noun "plates" is the antecedent of the pronoun "they.")

*An index to this entire Grammar Refresher section begins on page 167.

Avoid confusion by repeating the noun instead of using a pronoun if more than one noun might be considered to be the antecedent.

> The lamp hit the table when **the lamp** was knocked over.
> (Not: The lamp hit the table when **it** was knocked over.)

1c Verb

A **verb** is a word or group of words that **expresses action or being.**

> The plane **crashed** in Chicago. (action)

> Soccer **is** a popular sport. (being)

1d Adjective

An **adjective** is a word that **modifies a noun or pronoun.**

Note: In grammar, to modify a noun means to describe, talk about, explain, limit, specify, or change the character of a noun.

> Susan brought us **red** flowers.
> (The adjective "red" describes the noun "flowers.")

> Everyone at the party looked **beautiful.**
> (The adjective "beautiful" describes the pronoun "everyone.")

> **Several** people watched the parade.
> (The adjective "several" does not actually describe the noun "people"; it limits or talks about how many "people" watched the parade.)

> Those shoes are her **favorite** ones.
> (The adjective "favorite" defines or specifies which "ones.")

> They have **two** children.
> (The adjective "two" limits or specifies how many "children.")

1e Adverb

An **adverb** is a word that **modifies** the meaning of **a verb, an adjective, or another adverb.**

> The librarian spoke **softly.**
> (The adverb "softly" describes or explains how the librarian "spoke.")

> Jackie Onassis is **extremely** rich.
> (The adverb "extremely" talks about or specifies how "rich" Jackie Onassis is.)

> The job is **very** nearly completed.
> (The adverb "very" limits or specifies how "nearly" the job is completed.)

1f   Preposition

A **preposition** is a word that **connects a noun or pronoun to another word** in the sentence.

> The mayor campaigned **throughout** the city.
> (The preposition "throughout" connects the noun "city" to the verb "campaigned.")

A **preposition connects** a noun or pronoun to another word in the sentence **to show a relationship.**

> The wife **of** the oil executive was kidnapped.
>
> A friend **of** mine is a good lawyer.
>
> The strainer **for** the sink is broken.
>
> The floor **under** the sink is wet.
>
> David wants to work **in** the city.
>
> The accident occurred **about** eight o'clock.

1g   Conjunction

A **conjunction** is a word that **joins words, phrases, or clauses.**

> Alan's father **and** mother are divorced. (two words joined)
>
> *phrase*   *phrase*
> Is your favorite song at the end **or** in the middle of the record? (two phrases joined)
>
> You may swim in the pool **but** don't stay long. (two clauses joined)

(See Chapter 12 for a discussion of how prepositions and conjunctions act as connectives.)

1h   Interjection

An **interjection** is a word (or group of words) that **expresses surprise, anger, pleasure, or some other emotion.**

> **Aha!** I've caught you.
>
> **Oh no!** What have you done now?

An **interjection** has **no grammatical relation** to another word.

> **Ouch!** I've hurt myself.

1i **A word may belong to more than one part of speech,** depending on its meaning.

Example 1

Everyone **but** Sam was invited to the wedding. (preposition)

The Orioles won the pennant **but** the Angels came close to winning. (conjunction)

Harry has **but** ten dollars left in his bank account. (adverb)

Example 2

He lives **up** the street. (preposition)

It's time to get **up.** (adverb)

The sun is **up.** (adjective)

Every life has its **ups** and downs. (noun)

I'll **up** you five dollars. (verb)

Note: Just for fun—what is the part of speech of the word "behind" in this sentence?

Attempting to save Annie, the fireman ran for the door, dragging her **behind.**

Our answer is an adverb, meaning "at the rear." If your answer was a noun—Oh my! The noun means a certain part of the human body. We won't tell you which part.

CHAPTER 2
Clauses and Phrases

2a Clauses

A **clause** is a **group of words** within a sentence.

From his room, **he could see the park.** (one clause)

The children loved the man   **who sold ice cream.** (two clauses)

A clause contains a subject and a verb.

subject   verb

Before the race, **the jockeys inspected their horses.** (one clause)

subject   verb   subject   verb

When the   rain   stopped,   the air   was   cooler. (two clauses)

2b There are two types of clauses: **main** and **subordinate.***

main clause

During the riot, several people got hurt.

subordinate clause   main clause

When she won the lottery, Mrs. Ya-ching shouted with joy.

A **main clause** makes sense by itself.

We got the day off.

A **main clause** expresses a complete thought.

The fire was put out.
    (**Not:** When the fire was put out.)

It rained this morning.
    (**Not:** Because it rained this morning.)

A **subordinate clause** does not make sense by itself.

While the washing machine was broken, we couldn't wash anything.
    (The subordinate clause does not make sense without the rest of the
    sentence.)

Because a subordinate clause does not make sense by itself, a subordinate clause cannot stand as a complete sentence.

While the washing machine was broken. . . .

---

*A main clause may be called an independent clause. A subordinate clause may be called a
dependent clause.

A subordinate clause depends on a particular word in a main clause to make the subordinate clause mean something.

main clause   subordinate clause

Jack abandoned the car **which had two flat tires.**
    (The subordinate clause depends on the noun "car" in the main clause to describe the car.)

main clause   subordinate clause

The job was offered to Ann **because she was best qualified.**
    (The subordinate clause depends on the verb "was offered" in the main clause to explain **why** the job was offered.)

main clause   subordinate clause

My new neighbor is the one **who is waving.**
    (The subordinate clause depends on the pronoun "one" in the main clause to tell **who** is waving.)

A subordinate clause may be used in a sentence as an **adjective,** an **adverb** or a **noun.**

Woody Allen's new film is the funniest movie **that he has made yet.**
    (The subordinate clause acts like an adjective because it modifies —talks about—the noun "movie.")

The child giggled **while he was asleep.**
    (The subordinate clause functions like an adverb because it modifies the verb "giggled.")

Please tell me **what this is all about.**
    (The subordinate clause acts like a noun because it is the object of the action verb "tell.")

2c Phrases

A phrase is a group of words within a sentence.

Thurmon Munson died **in a plane crash.** (one phrase)

Let's sit **under that apple tree.** (one phrase)

At the top   **of the hill**   there were some cows grazing. (two phrases)

The phrase itself does not contain a subject or a verb.

subject   verb

Many streets **in the city** need repairs.

A phrase does not make sense by itself.

Ellen has a collection **of beautiful earrings.**
    (The phrase "of beautiful earrings" does not make sense by itself; therefore, the phrase cannot stand alone as a complete sentence.)

A phrase may begin with a preposition, a participle, a gerund, or an infinitive.

preposition
↓
Put the milk **into** **the refrigerator.** (prepositional phrase)

participle
↓
There are several people **waiting** **in line.** (participial phrase)

gerund
↓
Running ten miles a day is hard work. (gerund phrase)

infinitive
↓
To sing well take a lot of practice. (infinitive phrase)

A phrase may be used as **a noun,** an **adjective** an **adverb.**

A doctor's job is **to heal people.**
   (The infinitive phrase acts like a noun because it names the doctor's job.)

Raising his hands, the pope blessed the crowd.
   (The participial phrase acts like an adjective because it describes the pope.)

Most stores close **at five o'clock.**
   (The prepositional phrase acts like an adverb because it tells when most stores close.)

CHAPTER 3
The Sentence and Its Parts

3a   A **sentence** is a **group of words** that has a **subject** and a **verb.**

       subject   verb
       ↓   ↓
    The **concert began** at midnight.

               subject   verb
               ↓   ↓
    During the storm, the **electricity was knocked out.**

3b   A sentence may be **declarative, interrogative,** or **exclamatory.**

    A **declarative** sentence **states or asserts.**

        Inflation is a serious problem.

    An **interrogative** sentence **asks a question.**

        How long must we suffer?

    An **exclamatory** sentence **expresses emotion***

        What a fool he is!

    A **sentence** expresses a **complete thought.**

        The price of gold has gone up.

        Bus service will resume on Friday morning.

Note: Because a sentence expresses a complete thought, a sentence makes sense by itself.

        Peter likes to tend his vegetable garden. (complete thought)

        Peter likes. (incomplete thought—not a sentence)

        The gasoline shortage created serious problems. (complete thought)

        The gasoline shortage. (incomplete thought—not a sentence).

3c   **The four types of sentences according to structure are the following:**

    (1) **Simple**   Everyone likes music.

    (2) **Compound**   The Simons put their house up for sale on Friday, and it was sold by Monday.

*An "exclamatory sentence" is sometimes called an "imperative sentence."

(3) **Complex**   If you want good Szechuan cooking, you should

          go to the Hot Wok Restaurant.

(4) **Compound-Complex** Bob met Sally, who was in town for a few

          days, and they went to a museum.

3d Simple sentence

A **simple sentence** is made up of **one main clause** only.

> I love you.

A simple sentence may be of any length.

> The old man sitting on the park bench is the father of a dozen men and women besides being the grandfather of nearly forty children.

Note: A simple sentence **does not have a subordinate clause** in it.

3e Compound sentence

A **compound sentence** has **two or more main clauses.**

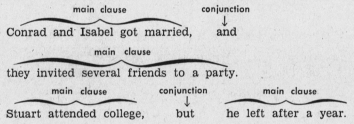

Each main clause in a compound sentence may stand by itself as a simple sentence—as long as the conjunction is left out.

>   conjunction
>   ↓
> Carlos will arrive by plane tonight, and Maria will go to the airport to meet him. (compound sentence)

> Carlos will arrive by plane tonight. (simple sentence)

> Maria will go to the airport to meet him. (simple sentence)

Note: A compound sentence does not have any subordinate clauses.

3f Complex sentence

A complex sentence contains only one main clause and one or more subordinate clauses.

>   subordinate clause   main clause
> After he signed the treaty, President Carter asked the Senate to ratify it. (one main clause and one subordinate clause)

subordinate clause *main clause*

Although they are expensive to install, solar heating systems save money

subordinate clause

and energy, which are hard to get these days. (one main clause and two subordinate clauses)

subordinate clause

Because he came from the planet Krypton,

main clause *subordinate clause*

Superman had special powers that no one on Earth could equal,

subordinate clause

though many people have tried.
(one main clause and three subordinate clauses)

3g   Compound-complex sentence

A compound-complex sentence is made up of **two or more main clauses and one or more subordinate clauses.**

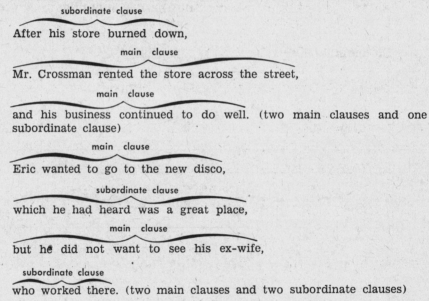

subordinate clause

After his store burned down,

main clause

Mr. Crossman rented the store across the street,

main clause

and his business continued to do well. (two main clauses and one subordinate clause)

main clause

Eric wanted to go to the new disco,

subordinate clause

which he had heard was a great place,

main clause

but he did not want to see his ex-wife,

subordinate clause

who worked there. (two main clauses and two subordinate clauses)

Note: For helpful guidance as to which sentence type to use, turn to "Vary Your Sentence Patterns," page 191.

3h   The parts of a sentence

The basic parts of a sentence are   a **subject,**   a **verb,**   and a **complement.***

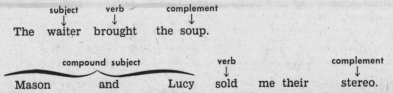

subject   *verb*   *complement*

The   waiter   brought   the soup.

compound subject   *verb*   *complement*

Mason   and   Lucy   sold   me their   stereo.

*The complement is discussed on pages 115-117.

3i   Subject

A **subject** of a sentence is the word (or group of words) that **tells who or what is being talked about.**

> **Ann Landers** gives advice to millions of Americans.
> (Because Ann Landers is being talked about, "Ann Landers" is the subject of the sentence.)

> High **taxes** caused many businesses to close.
> (Because we are told that high taxes caused businesses to close, the noun "taxes" is the subject of the sentence.)

> **Whoever goes to bed last** should shut off the lights.
> (Because we are told that whoever goes to bed last should do something, the noun clause "whoever goes to bed last" is the subject of the sentence.)

> **Brushing one's teeth and getting checkups regularly** are two important parts of good dental care.
> (Because brushing one's teeth and getting checkups are discussed, the two gerund phrases are the **compound subject** of the sentence.)

3j   A subject may be a **noun, pronoun, verbal, phrase, or clause.**

(1) A subject is usually a noun.

> Our **wedding** will be held outdoors.

> The **White House** is the home of the president.

> The **police** arrested the anti-nuclear energy demonstrators.

(2) A subject may be a pronoun.

> **He** always gets his way. (personal pronoun used as the subject)

> **Hers** is the tan raincoat. (possessive pronoun used as the subject)

> **What** did you do? (interrogative pronoun used as the subject)

> **That** is my car. (demonstrative pronoun used as the subject)

> **Everyone** was happy. (indefinite pronoun used as the subject)

(3) A subject may be a verbal.*

> **To begin** is the hardest part of the job. (infinitive used as the subject)

> **Jogging** is good exercise. (gerund used as a subject)

Note: A participle may not be used as a subject.

*See Chapter 8.

(4) A subject may be a **phrase.**

> **Smoking cigarettes** is unhealthy. (gerund phrase used as a subject)
>
> **To obey the law** is everyone's duty. (infinitive phrase used as a subject)

(5) A subject may be a subordinate **clause.**

> **Whatever you decide** is all right.
>
> **That Danny had cancer** saddened his friends.
>
> **What will happen** is going to surprise you.
>
> **Who will star in the movie** will be announced.

3k   Verb

A verb is a word or group of words that **usually tells what the subject does.**

> Annie **skated** down the street.
>
> Your baby **has dropped** his toy.
>
> President Nixon **resigned.**
>
> The telephone **is ringing.**

Two or more verbs may have one subject.

> They **defeated** the Cubs but **lost** to the Pirates.
>
> Dick **works** during the day and **goes** to school at night.

A verb may express a state or condition.

> Lynn **appears** puzzled. (Or: Lynn **appears to be** puzzled.)
>
> The stew **tastes** delicious.
>
> Jason and Martha **are** good friends.

3l   The three kinds of verbs are **transitive, intransitive,** and **linking.**

3m   A transitive verb tells what its subject does to someone or to something.

> The cat **caught** the mouse.
>
> Phil **washed** the dishes.
>
> Carol's mother **slapped** the boy.

3n An intransitive verb tells what its subject does. The action of the intransitive verb does not affect someone or something else.

The old man **slept** in his chair.

The audience **applauded**.

All of the job applicants **waited** patiently.

Note: Many verbs may be transitive or intransitive.

He **will return** the book tomorrow. (transitive)

The manager **will return** in an hour. (intransitive)

Whether a verb is transitive or intransitive depends on how it is used in the sentence.

Chuck **opened** the package.
(The verb is transitive because the action was carried out on something.)

The door **opened** slowly.
(The verb is intransitive because the action by the subject "door" did not affect anything else.)

3o A linking verb links the subject with a noun or a pronoun or an adjective.

"Jaws" was a terrifying **film**. (noun)

It's **I**.* (pronoun)

The child in this old photograph is **I**. (pronoun)

The girl who loves Peter is **she**. (pronoun)

The Beatles were **popular** in the 1960's. (adjective)

A linking verb may link the subject with an infinitive, a gerund, or a noun clause.

Stephanie's greatest pleasure is **to sing**. (infinitive)

Herb's mistake was **lying**. (gerund)

David's new job seemed **what he had hoped for**. (noun clause)

Linking verbs are to be, to appear, to grow, to seem, to remain, to become, and verbs that involve the senses, such as **to look, to smell, to feel, to sound,** and **to taste.**

Karen and Valerie **are** sisters.

Ben **is** strong.

---

*In spoken English, it is acceptable to say "It's me" or "It's us." It is not acceptable, however, to say "It's him," "It's her," or "It's them."

Eric **appears** healthy.

The situation at the prison **remains** tense.

Gertrude **feels** better.

Jim **sounds** angry.

A verb that appears to be a sense-linking verb may not actually be a sense-linking verb.

The milk **smells** sour. (linking verb)

The dog **smells** the fire hydrant. (transitive verb)

Tony **looked** sad. (linking verb)

Rosie **looked** through the window. (intransitive verb)

Note: The use of a particular verb determines whether that verb is sense-linking **or** transitive **or** intransitive.

3p

Transitive verb	Intransitive verb	Linking verb
1. Expresses action	1. Expresses action	1. Does not express action
2. Is followed by a direct object which receives the action subject / trans. verb / direct object ↓ ↓ ↓ Keith shot a deer.	2. Is not followed by a direct object subject / intrans. verb ↓ ↓ Jimmy grinned.	2. May be followed by a noun or an adjective subject / link. verb / predicate noun ↓ ↓ ↓ Juanita is a nurse subject / link. verb / predicate adjective ↓ ↓ ↓ Lenny looks sick.

CHAPTER 4
Verbs

4a **Five characteristics of every verb are   number,   person,   tense, mood,   and   voice.**

4b **Number shows whether the subject of the verb is singular or plural.**

Maggie **drives** well. (singular)

Adam and Peter **drive** dangerously. (plural)

Joan's grandmother **is** in Atlanta. (singular)

Arthur's parents **are** from Texas. (plural)

A verb must always agree in number with its subject.

subject   verb
↓   ↓
Emily   **lives** alone. (subject and verb both singular)

subject   subject   verb
↓   ↓   ↓
Dennis   and   Chuck   **live**   together. (subject and verb both plural)

4c **Person tells whether the subject of the verb is speaking, being spoken to, or being spoken about.**

I **am** the person in charge. (first person)

You **are** my best friend. (second person)

Bill **is** not here. (third person)

I **swim** at the YMCA. (first person)

You **come** with me. (second person)

Rosa **speaks** Spanish and French. (third person)

All three persons may be singular or plural in number.

	Singular	Plural
First person	I run	we run
Second person	you run	you run
Third person	he runs	
	she runs	they run
	it runs	

Note: The same verb form frequently is used for different persons and different numbers.

I love ice cream. (first person singular)
We love ice cream. (first person plural)
They love ice cream. (third person plural)

4d Tense shows when the action of the verb takes places—whether in the present, the past, or the future.

A plane **is passing** over our house right now. (present)

Our guests **are** here. (present)

Two U.S. astronauts **walked** on the moon in 1969. (past)

The workmen **were** here yesterday. (past)

We'll **pay** you tomorrow. (future)

Many people **will be** at the party tomorrow. (future)

4e Mood indicates how a sentence is used—whether it is a statement or a question, a command or a request, a wish or a condition.

Dinner **is** ready. (statement)

Does Elizabeth **work** in New Jersey? (question)

Go away! (command)

Please **pass** me the bread. (request)

If it **doesn't** rain, we can go. (condition)

The three kinds of moods are indicative, imperative, and subjunctive.

The indicative mood is used to express a statement or a question.

Two firemen were injured in the blaze. (statement)

Are you going out tonight? (question)

The imperative mood expresses a command or a request.

Turn off that radio! (command)

May I have a menu? (request—not question)

Note: The imperative mood is frequently indicated by leaving out the pronoun "you."

(You) Stop that!

The subjunctive mood may be used to show that a wish rather than a fact is being expressed.

I wish I **were** ten years younger.

4f Voice indicates whether the subject acts or is acted upon.

The dog **barked** at the stranger.

The baby **was kissed** several times.

A verb in the active voice shows that the subject is doing something.

The thieves **wounded** the bank teller. (active voice)

The curtains **blocked** out view. (active voice)

A verb in the passive voice shows that something is being done to the subject.

The garbage **was picked up** this morning. (passive voice)

Tyrone's car **is being washed.** (passive voice)

4g Complement

A complement may be one or more words that come after either a transitive or a linking verb.

                     complement
                        ↓
Fire destroyed the **building**. (transitive verb)

                  complement
                     ↓
The cat seemed **startled.** (linking verb)

                 complement   complement
                    ↓   ↓
Tony bought his **wife**   a silver **necklace.** (transitive verb)

              complement
                 ↓
Adam will be **president**   someday. (linking verb)

A complement completes the meaning of the verb.

The junta took **control of the government.**

A baseball broke the **window.**

4h The four ways that a complement may be used in a sentence are 1) as a direct object of the verb, 2) as an indirect object of the verb, 3) as a predicate noun,* and 4) as a predicate adjective.

Sally waters her **garden** every day. (direct object, receiving the action of the verb)

*A predicate noun is also called a predicate nominative.

Vincent gave his **brother** a basketball. (indirect object, telling to whom the action of the verb was directed)

Note: The noun "basketball" is the direct object of the transitive verb "gave"; therefore, "basketball" is also a complement.

Arthur Fiedler was the **conductor** of the Boston Pops. (predicate noun, renaming the subject after the linking verb)

Alaska is **huge.** (predicate adjective, describing the subject after the linking verb)

4i **A complement used as a direct object of the verb may be a noun, a pronoun, or a subordinate clause.**

Uncle Nate plants **vegetables** each spring. (noun used as direct object)

You should see **her** now. (pronoun used as direct object)

Tell me **what you know about life insurance.** (subordinate clause used as direct object)

4j **A complement used as an indirect object of the verb may also be a noun, a pronoun, or a subordinate clause.**

The nurse sent the **patient** a bill. (noun used as indirect object)

Will you do **me** a favor? (pronoun used as indirect object)

Give **whoever calls today** this information. (subordinate clause used as indirect object)

Note: From the three examples above, you can see that **an indirect object must always be accompanied by a direct object.**

The three sentences above—which have indirect objects—may be expressed in a different way.

The nurse sent a bill **to the patient.**

Will you do a favor **for me?**

Give this information to **whoever calls today.**

In these three sentences, the prepositional phrases serve the purpose of indirect objects.

4k   A complement that acts as a predicate noun may be a noun, a pronoun, a verbal, a phrase, or a clause.

Juan's uncle is a **bus driver.** (noun)

It is **she.** (pronoun)

Fred's favorite sport is **sailing.** (gerund)

President Sadat's desire is **to make peace.** (infinitive phrase)

Fixing cars is **what Tom does best.** (noun clause)

4l   A complement that acts like a predicate adjective may be an adjective or an adjective phrase.

Laverne and Shirley are **funny.** (adjective)

The lecture was **about alcoholism.** (adjective phrase)

Note: Both predicate nouns and predicate adjectives may be called predicate complements.

CHAPTER 5
Nouns and Pronouns

5a Nouns

The five types of nouns are **1) proper, 2) common, 3) collective, 4) concrete,** and **5) abstract.***

5b A proper noun names a particular person, place, or thing.

Cesar Chavez, San Clemente, Statue of Liberty
(Proper nouns always begin with a capital letter.)

5c A common noun names a general sort of person, place, or thing.

waitress, store, table

5d A collective noun names a group of individuals.

congregation, class, political party

(A collective noun is singular in form, but it refers to many people.)

5e A concrete noun names any material object that is inanimate.

apple, hat, ball, box, desk, book, shirt

5f An abstract noun names a quality, state, or idea.

truth, motion, beauty

5g Pronouns

The six kinds of pronouns are **1) personal, 2) relative, 3) interrogative, 4) indefinite, 5) demonstrative,** and **6) reflexive.**

5h A personal pronoun stands for the speaker, the person spoken to, or the person or thing spoken about.

I am going out.
(The first person "I" is speaking.)

You should see the traffic jam downtown.
(The second person "you" is being spoken to.)

She wants to become a lawyer.
(The third person "she" is being spoken about.)

---

*A noun may be of more than one type. For example, "table" is both a common noun and a concrete noun.

The **personal pronouns** are the following:

>   I, you, he, she, it, we, they, me, us, him, her, them

The **possessive** forms of the personal pronouns are the following:

>   my, mine, yours, his, hers, its, our, ours, their, theirs

A pronoun should be in the same person as the noun or pronoun it refers to.

> The tree was damaged when lightning struck **it**. (noun and pronoun in third person)

> **Everyone** knows that **he** should dress well to make a good impression. (both pronouns in third person)
>   (Not: **Everyone** knows that **you** should . . .)

5i   The **relative pronouns** are the following:

>   who (whom), which, what, that

A relative pronoun may begin a subordinate clause.

> The child, **who** was alone, looked unhappy.

A relative pronoun connects the main clause to the subordinate clause.

> The problem was in the gas line, **which** was rusty.
>   (The relative pronoun "which" joins the main clause to the subordinate clause it begins.)

A relative pronoun stands for a noun in the main clause.

> Sharon gave me the money **that** I needed.
>   (The relative pronoun "that" stands for the noun "money" in the main clause.)

When to use the relative pronoun "whom"

"Whom" is the objective case form of "who." We use "whom" as a **direct object,** an **indirect object,** or an **object of the preposition.**

> The men **whom** you see are waiting for work.
>   (The relative pronoun "whom" is the direct object of the verb "see.")

> Hansen is the person to **whom** Wilmot gave the bribe money.
>   (The relative pronoun "whom" is the indirect object of the verb "gave.")

> The typewriter was stolen by the messenger about **whom** the office manager had been suspicious.
>   (The relative pronoun "whom" is the object of the preposition "about.")

5j   An interrogative pronoun asks a question.

> **Who** wants to start first?
>
> **What** did Richard do then?
>
> **Which** should I take?
>
> **Whose** is this jacket?
>
> **Whom** do you want to speak to?

5k   An indefinite pronoun refers to a number of persons, places, or things in a general way.

> **None** of the dishes was broken.
>
> Mark finds **everything** about boats interesting.
>
> I'll bring you **another**.
>
> **Some** of my friends buy lottery tickets.

Other commonly used indefinite pronouns are the following:

> any, both, few, many, most, one, other, several, such

5l   A demonstrative pronoun points out a specific person or thing.

> **This** is not my handwriting.
>
> May I have two of **those**?
>
> **That** is my brother.
>
> **These** are my best friends.

Note: Interrogative, indefinite, and demonstrative pronouns may be used as adjectives.

> **Which** dessert do you want? (interrogative adjective)
>
> **Every** time I try to skate I fall down. (indefinite adjective)
>
> **That** dress costs too much. (demonstrative adjective)

5m   A reflexive pronoun refers back to the noun it stands for.

> I hurt **myself** while jogging.
>
> Amy considers **herself** an adult.

A reflexive pronoun may be the **direct object of a verb**, the **indirect object of a verb**, the **object of a preposition**, or a **predicate noun**.

Kim pushed **himself** and finished the race. (direct object)

Ray brought **himself** a new watch. (indirect object)

Buffie likes to be by **herself**. (object of a preposition)

Mr. Thompson is just not **himself** lately. (predicate nominative)

Note: Do not use "hisself" for "himself," or "theirselves' for "themselves."

5n   Three characteristics shared by all nouns and pronouns are gender, number, and case.

5o   Gender indicates the sex of the person or thing named—whether masculine, feminine, or neuter.

Adam wants some ice cream, but **he** is on a diet.
. ("Adam" and the pronoun "he" are both masculine in gender.)

Alice said **she** was ready.
("Alice" and the pronoun "she" are both feminine in gender.)

The **movie** was good, but **it** was too long.
("Movie" and the pronoun "it" are neither masculine nor feminine; therefore, they are both neuter in gender.)

A pronoun should be in the same gender as the noun it refers to.

5p   Number indicates whether one or more than one person or thing is named.

Here is a **letter** for you.
(The one letter is singular in number.)

Many **cars** were involved in the accident.
(Many "cars" are plural in number.)

Note: A collective noun is singular in form, but usually plural in meaning.

The audience was upset by the delay.
("Audience" in singular in number, although many people are in the audience.)

A pronoun should be in the same number as the noun it refers to.

The **dishes** are not clean, so don't use **them**.
("Dishes" and the pronoun "them" are both plural in number.)

Hockey is a lot of fun, but **it** is rough.
("Hockey" and the pronoun "it" are both singular in number.)

A pronoun that refers to a collective noun that is considered as a unit should be singular in number.

The home team won **its** final game of the season.

A pronoun that refers to a collective noun that is considered as a group of individuals should be plural.

The visiting team felt **they** deserved to win.

A pronoun that refers to an indefinite pronoun antecedent must be singular.

Almost anyone can earn a good living if **he** or **she** works hard.

A pronoun must be singular if it refers to singular antecedents joined by "or" or "nor."

Neither Earle nor Jeff could find **his** coat.

5q **Case shows how a noun or pronoun is used in a sentence.**

They stayed out all night.
("They" is the subject.)

Natalie knew **him**.
("Him" is the object of the transitive verb.)

Craig thinks this hat is **his**.
("His" is a pronoun that shows ownership.)

The three cases are nominative, objective, and possessive.

5r **The nominative case names the subject of a verb or the predicate noun of a linking verb.**

Susan and **I** will call you tonight. (subjects)

My best friends are **Katherine** and **you**. (predicate nouns)

A noun in the nominative case usually is placed before a verb.

Mr. Garcia opened a dry cleaning business.

Ida answered the telephone.

Personal pronouns in the nominative case have the following forms:

I, you, he, she, it, we, they

The subject of a subordinate clause must be in the nominative case even if the clause itself acts as a direct object or an object of a preposition.

Show me **who** is waiting to see me. (subordinate clause as direct object)

Discuss this form with **whoever** applies for the job. (subordinate clause as object of a preposition)

5s **The objective case indicates that nouns and pronouns act as direct objects, indirect objects, or objects of prepositions.**

The storm forced **them** to stay home. (direct object)

Victor enjoyed meeting **her.** (direct object)

Sally called **us, Mary and me, into her office.** (direct objects)

The cab driver gave **me** good directions. (indirect object)

Our supervisor showed **him** and **me** some contracts. (indirect objects)

Annette had trouble teaching **them** how to type. (indirect object)

Several of **us** want more food. (object of the preposition)

Between **you** and **me, I** don't like our boss. (objects of the preposition)

Note: Each noun or pronoun in a compound object must be in the objective case.

A noun is in the objective case if it is placed after a transitive verb or after a preposition.

He saw **Greta Garbo.**

Ernie went into the **store.**

Personal pronouns in the objective case have the following forms:

me, you, him, her, it, us, them

5t Only two personal pronouns "**we**" ("**us**") and "**you**"—may also be used as **adjective pronouns.**

We women have responded to the challenge of the 1980's.

They are discriminating against **us** women.

You boys should play more quietly.

Note: The adjective pronoun "we" is in the nominative case when it modifies a subject. The adjective pronoun "us" is in the objective case when it modifies an object of a verb or an object of a preposition.

We Democrats support President Carter's bid for re-election. (nominative case when modifying subject)

Mom sent **us** children to bed. (objective case when modifying direct object of verb)

Won't you give **us** boys a chance to earn some money? (objective case when modifying indirect object of verb)

Many Orientals were on the plane with **us** Americans. (objective case when modifying object of a preposition)

5u The objective case is used by nouns and pronouns that are the subject of an infinitive.

Paul's father wants **him** to help paint the house.

Should Fred ask **her** to join the club?

A noun or pronoun following the infinitive **to be** must, like its subject, be in the objective case.

Pat didn't expect my friend to be **him**.

Note: If the infinitive **to be** has no subject, the noun or pronoun that comes after the infinitive is in the nominative case.

My twin brother is often thought to be **I**. (nominative case)

5v The possessive case indicates ownership.

Martha's home is in Ohio.

This book is **mine**.

Possession is generally shown by using an apostrophe:

Bumbry's error   men's room

child's toy   ship's crew

Ownership may be shown by an "of" phrase.

The handle **of the door** is broken.

The "of" phrase is used in formal English to show possession by inanimate things or to avoid awkward constructions.

The passage **of the bill** now in Congress will mean lower taxes.
    Not: The bill's passage. . . .)

The sister **of my uncle's wife** is eighty years old.
    (Not: My uncle's wife's sister. . . .)

Personal and relative pronouns have distinct forms to show the possessive case.

The following are personal pronouns (possessive form):

> my, mine, your, yours, his, her, hers, our, ours, their, theirs, its*

That dress is **hers.**

Ours is the house on the left.

"Whose" is a relative pronoun (possessive form.)*

No one knows **whose** it is.

The possessive forms **my, your, his, our, their,*** and **whose** are called adjective pronouns because they modify nouns.

Your shirt has a button missing.

My family is very large.

Their apartment costs a lot of money.

The woman **whose** typewriter I borrowed, gave it to me.

The possessive case is used by nouns and pronouns that come before a gerund.

Buba's shouting attracted a large crowd. (noun)

My being sick caused me to miss an important lecture. (pronoun)

The possessive case of a compound noun is indicated by adding 's to the **last word of the compound noun.**

A **movie star's** life is glamorous.

The **Governor of California's** speech attacked the president.

Pope John Paul II's visit to the United States pleased millions.

Note: **The plural of a compound noun** is formed by adding to the principal noun.

chief of police (singular)	chief of police's (singular possessive)
chiefs of police (plural)	chiefs of police's (plural possessive)

---

*"Its" is the possessive form of the personal pronoun "it." "It's" is a contraction of "it is."

"Whose" is the possessive form of the relative pronoun "who"; "who's" is a contraction of "who is."

"Their" is the possessive form of the relative pronoun "they"; "they're" is a contraction of "they are."

5w An **appositive** is a **noun or pronoun** usually placed next to another noun or pronoun to rename it.

> Two guys, **Nestar and his cousin**, were already there. (identifies the subject)

> Clarinda's dog **Sonya** eats only hamburgers. (renames the subject)

Note: An appositive must always be in the same case as the noun it renames.

> We, **my brother and I**, are going hunting together. (both subject and appositive in nominative case)

> Uncle Joe gave us, **Stuart and me**, tickets to the World Series. (both object and appositive in case)

5x **Direct address** and **nominative absolute** constructions are **always in the nominative case.**

Direct address consists of a noun (or pronoun) which names a particular person when someone else addresses that person.

> **Willy**, please come here immediately.

A nominative absolute consists of a noun plus a participle.

> **The money having been spent**, the boys decided to go home.

CHAPTER 6
Subject-Verb Relationship

6a A verb must agree with its subject in number and in person.

> Dr. Shu has office hours from 8 until 4.
> (The third person singular form of "to have" agrees with the subject "Dr. Shu.")

> Robin I **play** squash every Tuesday.
> (The first person plural form of "to play" agrees with the compound subject "Robin and I.")

6b Collective nouns are followed by singular or plural verbs according to the sense of the sentence.

> The jury **has** asked for more time.
> (The third person singular is used because the jury is considered to be a unified body.)

> The jury **are** unable to agree.
> (The third person plural is used because the jury is considered to be a group of twelve persons.)

To summarize, a **collective noun** is **singular** when it refers to a group as a single unit.

> A minority in Congress **is** delaying passage of the bill.

A **collective noun** is **plural** when it refers to the individual members of the group.

> A minority of Congressmen **want** to defeat the bill.

6c Some indefinite pronouns are always singular in meaning.

> **Each** of the candidates **wants** an opportunity to discuss his beliefs.

> **Anyone** is allowed to use the public beach.

> **Any one** of us is willing to help.

Some indefinite pronouns are always plural in meaning.

> **Many** of the drawings **were** beautiful.

> **A few** of the windows **were** broken.

> **Several** of Joe's friends **are** sorry that he left.

6d A verb should be singular if its subject has "every" or "many a" just before it.

> **Many a woman feels** entitled to more in life than just housework.

> **Every man, woman, and child wants** to be happy.

Some **indefinite pronouns** may be **singular or plural,** depending on the meaning of the sentence.

> **Some** of the books **have** been lost.
>
> **Some** of the work **was** completed.
>
> **All** of the ice cream **is** gone.
>
> **All** of the men **have** left.
>
> **Most** of the talk **was** about football.
>
> **Most** of the people **were** dissatisfied.

6e **When singular subjects are joined by "or" or "nor," the subject is considered to be singular.**

> **Neither** the mother **nor** her daughter **was** ever seen again.
>
> **One** or the **other** of us **has** to buy the tickets.

6f **When one singular and one plural subject are joined by "or" or "nor," the subject closer to the verb determines the number of the verb.**

> Neither the plumber nor the painters **have** finished.
>
> Either the branch offices or the main office **closes** at 4.

6g **When the subjects joined by "or" or "nor" are of different persons, the subject nearer the verb determines the person.**

> She or you **are** responsible.
>
> You or she **is** responsible.

To avoid such awkward sentences, place a verb next to each subject.

> Either she **is** responsible or you **are.**
>
> Either you **are** responsible or she **is.**

6h **Even if the verb comes before the subject, the verb agrees with the true subject in number and person.**

> **Are** the cat and the dog fighting? (The cat and the dog are. . . .)
>
> Coming at us from the left **was** an ambulance. (An ambulance was. . . .)
>
> There **are** two things you can do.* (Two things are. . . .)
>
> There **is** only one bottle left.* (Only one bottle is. . . .)

---

*In this sentence, *there* is an expletive. An expletive is a word that gets a sentence started, but it is not a subject. Another expletive is *it.*

6i **Interrogative pronouns and the adverbs "where," "here," and "there" do not affect the number or person of the verb when they introduce a sentence.**

subject
↓
What **is** the **name** of your friend?

subject
↓
What **are** the **addresses** of some good restaurants?

subject
↓
Who **is** the **man** standing over there?

subject
↓
Who **are** those **people?**

subject
↓
Here **comes** my **friend.**

subject
↓
Here **come** my **parents.**

6j **When a predicate noun (following a linking verb) differs in number from the subject, the verb must agree with the subject.**

Our biggest problem **is** angry customers.

More gas guzzlers **aren't** what this country needs.

6k **Parenthetical phrases** or other modifiers that come between the subject and verb **do not change the number or person of the true subject**—which the verb agrees with.

The amount shown, plus interest, **is** due on Friday.

The president, together with his advisers, **is** at Camp David.

CHAPTER 7
Tense

7a   Tense specifies the moment of an action or condition.

We **are walking** to the park. (present moment)

We **will walk** to the park tomorrow. (future moment)

We **walked** to the park yesterday. (past moment)

I **have worked** here for three years. (action begun in the past and continued into the present)

I **had worked** in Chicago for four years before I left. (past action completed **before** another past action)

I **will have worked** here six months next Friday. (past action to be completed sometime in the future)

7b   The six tenses are present, past, future, present perfect, past perfect, and future perfect.

7c   The present tense shows that an action is happening in the present or that a condition exists now.

I **live** here. (action)

He **is** busy now. (condition)

The **present tense** forms of **to work, to have,** and **to be** follow:

to work	to have	to be
I work	I have	I am
you work	you have	you are
he / she / it works	he / she / it has	he / she / it is
we work	we have	we are
you work	you have	you are
they work	they have	they are

The present tense may indicate **habitual action** or **habitual condition,** or **a general truth.**

Judy **leaves** her office every day at 5 o'clock. (habitual action)

Dana **is** allergic to chocolate. (habitual condition)

Two and two **are** four. (general truth)

The present tense may express **future time with the help of an adverb.**

adverb
↓
Gary flies to Washington **tomorrow**.

adverb
↓
We are going to see a movie **tonight**.

7d The **present perfect tense** shows that an action which **began in the past** is **still going on in the present.**

Betsy and I **have been** in New York for two years. (and are still in New York)

The Johnson family **has owned** a plumbing supply company for sixty years. (and still owns it)

The **present perfect tense** may show that an action **begun in the past was just completed at the present time.**

Our men have worked on your car until now.

Charlayne has just walked in.

The **present perfect tense** is formed with **have or has and a past participle.**

I **have eaten** too much.

Nina **has** always **loved** music.

7e The **past tense** shows that an action **occurred some time in the past** but has **not continued into the present.**

Laura's doctor **advised** her to lose weight.

The plane **landed** on time.

Susan **was living** in Philadelphia then. (progressive form)

We **went** along for the ride.

If the verb in the main clause is in the past tense, the verb in the subordinate clause must also be in the past tense.

The surgeon told his patient that an operation **was** necessary.
(**Not**: The surgeon told his patient that an operation **will be** necessary.)

Lenny said that he **would meet** Frank at 7:30.
(**Not**: Lenny said that he **will meet** Frank at 7:30.)

The past tense (first, second, and third person — singular and plural) is often formed by adding "ed" to the infinitive (without "to.")

Jim **helped** us many times.

We **called** you last night.

7f The **past perfect tense** indicates that an **action was completed before another action began.**

> I remembered the answer after **I had handed in** my exam.

> Kenny **had bought** the tickets before he met Ruth.

> Margaret **had worked** very hard, so she took a vacation.

Note: The **past tense** shows that an event happened at any time in the past, but the **past perfect tense** indicates that an event happened before another event in the past.

> Paula **had finished** dressing before I woke up.
> (Not: Paula **finished** dressing before I woke up.)

> Jake **had** already **left** by the time I arrived.)
> (Not: Jake already **left** by the time I arrived.)

The past perfect tense is formed with "had" and a past participle.

> Peter **had said** he would call before twelve.

7g The **future tense** indicates that an **action is going to take place sometime in the future.**

> All of us **will pay** more for heat this winter.

> The weatherman says it **will rain** tomorrow.

> **Will** you **join** us for lunch, Eric?

> **I'll go** away this weekend.

The future tense is formed with "will" and the infinitive (without "to").

> Don **will take** you to the airport.

7h The **future perfect tense** is used to express a **future action that will be completed before another future action.**

> By the time we get home,* my parents **will have gone** to bed.

> We'll start eating after you **(will) have washed** your hands.
> Helena **will have finished** her work when we meet her at the office.

The future perfect tense is formed with "will have" and a past participle.

> Patty **will have quit** her job by Christmas.

*See page 131 (top), which discusses how a present tense may express future time.

7i **All six tenses may be expressed in a progressive form by adding a present participle of a verb to the appropriate form of "to be."**

The Cosmos **are winning.** (present progressive)

The Cosmos **were winning.** (past progressive)

The Cosmos **have been winning.** (present perfect progressive)

The Cosmos **had been winning.** (past perfect progressive)

The Cosmos **will be winning.** (future progressive)

The Cosmos **will have been winning.** (future perfect progressive)

7j **Principal parts of irregular verbs**

We call a verb like "eat" an irregular verb. Any verb that changes internally to form the past participle is an iregular verb.

Present Tense	Past Tense	Past Participle	Present Participle
eat	ate	eaten	eating
begin	began	begun	beginning
blow	blew	blown	blowing
break	broke	broken	breaking
burst	burst	burst	bursting
catch	caught	caught	catching
choose	chose	chosen	choosing
come	came	come	coming
do	did	done	doing
drink	drank	drunk	drinking
drive	drove	driven	driving
fall	fell	fallen	falling
find	found	found	finding
fly	flew	flown	flying
freeze	froze	frozen	freezing
give	gave	given	giving
go	went	gone	going
grow	grew	grown	growing
know	knew	known	knowing
lay (placc)	laid	laid	laying
lie (rest)	lay	lain	lying
ring	rang	rung	ringing
raise	raised	raised	raising
rise	rose	risen	rising
run	ran	run	running
set	set	set	setting
sit	sat	sat	sitting
speak	spoke	spoken	speaking
steal	stole	stolen	stealing
swim	swam	swum	swimming
take	took	taken	taking
throw	threw	thrown	throwing
wear	wore	worn	wearing
write	wrote	written	writing

CHAPTER 8
Verbals

8a   A verbal is a word formed from a verb.

> **Skiing** can be dangerous.
>
> We could hear our neighbors **arguing**.
>
> Bonnie and Clyde worked hard **to succeed**.

8b   The three kinds of verbals are gerunds, participles, and infinitives.

8c   A gerund acts like a noun.

> **Smoking** is not allowed in many stores.
>
> **Traveling** by train can be fun.
>
> Mark's favorite sport is **boating**.

A gerund ends in "ing."

> Nureyev's **dancing** is terrific.
>
> **Flying** is the fastest way to get there.

A phrase that begins with a gerund is called a gerund phrase.

> **Paying bills** on time is a good habit.
>
> **Leaving my friends** made me sad.

8d   A participle acts like an adjective.

> The police stopped the **speeding** car.
>
> The **tired** children were sent to bed.

A present participle ends in "ing."

> A priest comforted the **dying** woman.
>
> **Running**, the girl caught up with her friends.

Note: A present participle looks like a gerund because they both end in "ing." A present participle, however, is used as an adjective, not as a noun.

A past participle usually ends in "d," "ed," "t," "n," or "en."

Used clothing is cheaper than new clothes.

Woody left **written** instructions for his assistant.

A phrase that begins with a participle is called a participial phrase.

Getting off the elevator, I met a friend.

Questioned by the police, several witnesses described the robbery.

8e   An infinitive is used as a noun or an adjective or an adverb.

Franz loves **to dance.** (noun)

Our candidate has the ability **to win.** (adjective)

Lisa practices every day **to improve.** (adverb)

An infinitive usually begins with "to," but not always.

Sally wants **to know** if you need a ride.

Help me wash my car. (Or: Help me **to wash** my car.)

A phrase introduced by an infinitive is called an infinitive phrase.

His only desire was **to save money.** (infinitive phrase used as a noun)

There must be a way **to solve this problem.** (infinitive phrase used as an adjective)

The doctor is too busy **to see you now.** (infinitive phrase used as an adverb)

8f   Gerunds may be present or perfect.

Good **cooking** is her specialty. (present)

Your **having arrived** on time saved me. (perfect)

A gerund in the present form refers to an **action happening at the same time as the action of the main verb.**

Swimming is fun.

Running a mile tired him out.

Taking driving lessons will help you drive better.

A gerund in the perfect form refers to an **action that was completed before the time of the main verb.**

He believes his recovery is a result of his **having prayed.**

Our **having read** the book made the movie boring.

8g   Participles may be present, past, or perfect.

The woman **sitting** on the couch is my mother. (present)

Warned by his doctor, Jack began to exercise. (past)

Having been recognized, Elton John was mobbed by his fans. (perfect)

A present participle refers to action happening at the same time as the action of the main verb.

present
↓
Smiling broadly, the president **answers** questions from the audience.

past
↓
Smiling broadly, the president **answered** questions from the audience.

present
↓
Holding up his hands, the teacher **is asking** for silence.

past
↓
Holding up his hands, the teacher **asked** for silence.

A past participle sometimes refers to action happening at the same time as the action of the main verb.

Irritated by his sister, Raphael yelled at her.

Dressed up, Tom looks like a new man.

A past participle sometimes refers to action that happened before the action of the main verb.

Burned by the sun, Mary is suffering.

Awakened by the noise, we looked outside.

The perfect participle always refers to action occurring before the action of the main verb.

Having finished work, we can leave.

Having seen that movie, we went somewhere else.

Having left home in a hurry, Michael forgot his raincoat.

8h   Infinitives may be present or perfect.

Albert likes **to read** all day. (present)

Tina was supposed **to have brought** the money. (perfect)

The present infinitive shows an action occurring at the same time as the action of the main verb.

> **I am trying to finish** this puzzle. (both present)
>
> Jerry **looked** around **to see** who was there. (both past)
>
> Dana **will call to ask** you for some advice. (both future)

The present infinitive may indicate action or a state of being at some future time.

> I hope **to see** you again.
>
> I expect **to be** there in an hour.
>
> He intended **to write** to us.

An infinitive is never used in a subordinate clause which begins with "that."

> I expect everyone to remain seated.
>
> I expect that everyone will remain seated.
> (**Not:** I expect that everyone to remain seated.)

The perfect infinitive expresses action occurring before that of the main verb.

> I am sorry not **to have met** you before.
>
> He claims **to have seen** a flying saucer.

Avoid using the perfect infinitive after main verbs in the past or past perfect tense.

> I had expected **to receive** my mail today.
> (**Not:** I had expected **to have received.** . . .)
>
> They hoped **to join** us for dinner.
> (**Not:** They hoped **to have joined** us. . . .)
>
> Mike would have liked to ask Alice for a date, but he was too shy.
> (**Not:** Mike would have like **to have asked** Alice. . . .)

CHAPTER 9
Mood and Voice

9a   Mood

The **three moods** that a verb may express are **indicative, imperative,** and   **subjunctive.**

9b   The indicative mood indicates that the action or state is something believed to be true.

> **I am** the greatest.
>
> She **sings** beautifully.

The **indicative** mood is **used in asking a question.**

> **Are** you Mr. Feldman?
>
> **Does** Tom **want** to watch "Saturday Night Live"?

9c   The imperative mood expresses a command or a request or a suggestion.

> **Answer** the telephone. (command)
>
> **Give** me a napkin, please. (request)
>
> **Try** turning the handle the other way. (suggestion)

The imperative mood is not only more emphatic than the indicative mood—it is more quickly and easily understood.

> Give me that letter. (imperative)
>
> I would appreciate it if you would give me that letter. (indicative)

9d   The subjunctive mood is often used to express a wish or a condition that is not real—that is, contrary to fact.

> I wish the weather **were** nicer.
>
> If this paint **were** dry, we could sit on the bench.
>
> Debbie suggested that Carol **stay** at her apartment.
>
> Carl asked that Stan **agree** to pay for the damage.

The subjunctive mood is also used to express purpose or intention.

> Connie said that she **would visit** her mother at Easter.
>   (**Not:** Connie said that she **will visit** her mother at Easter.)
>
> We made box lunches so that we **would have** food for the trip.
>   (**Not:** We made box lunches so that we **had** food for the trip.)

The subjunctive mood is mainly indicated by **two forms of the verb "to be."** The forms are **"be"** and **"were."**

Be good.

If I **were** president, I'd nationalize the oil industry.

The present subjunctive uses "be" for all three persons, both singular and plural.

I be, you be, he be, we be, they be

I have one wish—that I **be** president some day.

Mrs. Diggs insists that you **be** given a bonus.

I asked that the child not **be** punished.

The judge ordered that the tenants **be** allowed to stay.

The more common form of the subjunctive is the past subjunctive form "were" for all three persons, both singular and plural.

If $\begin{Bmatrix} I \\ you \\ he \\ we \\ they \end{Bmatrix}$ **were** here, everything would be all right.

The subjunctive mood for verbs other than "to be" is formed by using the present tense first person singular form for all persons.

Mary suggested that Ronald **keep** an extra pair of eyeglasses.

The umpire insisted that the manager **leave** the field.

9e **Choosing between the subjunctive and indicative mood.**

One should show how he sees a situation: **contrary to fact or within the realm of possibility.** He does this by choosing either the subjunctive mood or the indicative mood.

If his statement **be** true, this is a case of fraud. (subjunctive)
(One indicates that he thinks it is highly improbable that the statement is true.)

If his statement **is** true, this may be a case of fraud. (indicative)
(The writer indicates that it is quite possible that the statement may be true.)

If he **were** at the meeting, he would. . . .) (subjunctive)
(The speaker tells the listener that the man is not at the meeting.)

If he **was** at the meeting, he would have been able to speak to the point. (indicative)
(Perhaps the man **was** at the meeting; one doesn't know.)

Had the first payment **been made** in April, the second would be due in September. (subjunctive)
> (The speaker indicates that the payment was **not** made in April.)

If the first payment **was** made in April, the second will be due in September. (indicative)
> (Perhaps it was made; perhaps not—the speaker doesn't know.)

Do not use "would have" instead of "had" in "if" clauses to express the past perfect tense of the subjunctive.

If he **had worked** harder, he would have a better job.
(Not: If he **would have worked** harder. . . .)

9f Voice

A verb is either in the active voice or in the passive voice.

9g A verb in the active voice indicates that the subject performs an action.

Maggie **reads** every night before going to sleep.

The fire **burned** the entire house.

A verb in the active voice stresses the subject or actor rather than the action.

9h A verb in the passive voice indicates that something is being done to the subject.

The children **were given** lunches to take to school.

The television **was turned** off by my dad

A verb in the passive voice stresses the action rather than the actor.

9i All transitive verbs—verbs whose action affects something or someone—can be used in the passive voice.

Johnny Bench **caught** the ball. (active)

The ball **was caught** by Johnny Bench. (passive)

9j **To form the passive,** the object of the transitive verb in the active voice is moved ahead of the verb, thus becoming the subject. A form of "to be" is added to the main verb. The subject of the active sentence is either left out or expressed in a prepositional phrase.

subject   active verb   direct object

The **tow truck pulled** the car out of the ditch. (active voice)

subject   passive verb   prepositional phrase

The **car was pulled** out of the ditch **by the tow truck.** (passive voice)

9k **If the active sentence has an indirect object as well as a direct object, either the indirect object or the direct object may be the subject of the passive sentence.**

active verb   indirect object   direct object

Tom **gave** his   **sister**   a **kitten.** (active)

subject   passive verb

A **kitten was given** by Tom to his sister. (passive)

subject   passive verb

Tom's **sister was given** a kitten by Tom. (passive)

9l **The passive voice is appropriate** to express an action **when the actor is unknown.**

The door had been locked before we arrived.

Note: In general, avoid the passive voice for clearer, more forceful sentences.

CHAPTER 10

Modifiers – Adjectives, Adjective Phrases and Clauses

10a Modifiers

A modifier adds information to another word in the sentence.

Blue flowers were growing in the field.
(The adjective "blue" adds color to the noun "flowers.")

Vera paints **beautifully.**
(The adverb "beautifully" tells how Vera paints.)

10b Modifiers may be a word, a phrase, or a clause.

Billy put on a **clean** shirt. (word)

The wristband **of her watch** was broken. (phrase)

Andy liked the painting **that was done by his friend.** (clause)

There are **various types** of modifiers.

Jill brought us **fresh** fruit. (adjective as modifier)

Bob's friends greeted him **warmly.** (adverb as modifier)

Rudy enjoyed the ride **from Birmingham to Atlanta.** (adjective phrase as modifier)

The rent will increase **after this month.** (adverb phrase as modifier)

Louise holds two jobs **because she supports her sons in college.** (subordinate clause as adverbial modifier)

The houses **where American presidents were born** are museums. (subordinate clause as adjectival modifier)

10c Adjectives modify nouns

The six kinds of adjectives are the following:

Limiting: Many children are bused to school.

Numerical: Four days have passed since I saw her.

Descriptive: Striped wallpaper hung in the hall.

Proper: American and **Russian** flags lined the parade route.

Pronoun: My book has a torn cover.

Article: A letter has arrived.

10d Articles

The **articles "a" and "an"** (indefinite articles) indicate that the **noun they modify is an example of a general type.**

A dove symbolizes peace. (any dove)

A doctor saves lives. (any doctor)

An ambulance brings people to hospitals (any ambulance)

Note: Do not use the articles "a' or "an" after "kind of," "type of," or "sort of."

A mango is **a kind of fruit.**
(Not: . . . **a kind of a fruit**)

The Citation is **a new type of car.**
(Not: . . . **a new type of a car.**)

That sound gives me **a sort of weird feeling.**
(Not: . . . **a sort of a weird feeling.**)

The article "the" (definite article) indicates that the noun it modifies is a particular noun.

The winner received ten thousand dollars. (specific person)

The lamp over there is sold. (specific thing)

10e Single adjectives and compound adjectives

A single adjective usually comes immediately before the word it modifies.

Help me carry this **heavy** package.

A compound adjective consists of **two or more words serving as a single adjective.**

The drought made the earth **bone dry.**

My dictionary is **up to date.**

When a compound adjective comes before a noun, the words are **joined by a hyphen.**

Woody Allen was my **next-door** neighbor.

A **large-scale** map is hanging on the wall.

When the modifying words follow a noun, they are not hyphenated, unless they are normally hyphenated compounds.

This book is **well written.**

My new watch is **self-winding.** (normally hyphenated)

When two or more adjectives come before a noun but do not act jointly, they are not hyphenated.

Jim was wearing a white silk shirt.

I've had a long, hard day.

Note: If the word "and" can be inserted between two adjectives that come before a noun without destroying the meaning of the sentence, put a comma in between the two adjectives; otherwise, do not.

Miss Cameron is a kind, generous person. (kind **and** generous)

Show us your new suit.

(**Not:** . . . your, new suit.)

10f   Two or more adjectives may follow the word they modify to make the sentence read more smoothly.

The children, **tired and hungry,** were difficult to control.

10g   Most adjectives may show greater or lesser degrees of their characteristic quality.

Today was **cold.** (characteristic quality)

Tomorrow will be **colder** than today. (greater)

The day after will be the **coldest.** (still greater)

Yesterday was **less cold** than today. (lesser)

The day before was the **least cold** this week. (lesser still)

Some adjectives do not show comparison.

Jennifer is **pregnant.**
     (She cannot be **more** or **less** pregnant.)

This salad dressing is **perfect.**
     (**Not:** . . . is **more** or **less** perfect.)

10h   The three degrees of comparison are positive, comparative, and superlative.

Tania is **happy.** (positive degree)

Lenny is **happier** than Frank. (comparative degree)

Wayne is the **happiest** of all. (superlative degree)

The positive degree simply names the quality expressed by an adjective.

I like **spicy** food.

The **comparative degree** indicates that the quality described by an adjective exists in one person to a **greater or lesser degree** than in another person or thing.

> Susan looks **older** than Liz. (greater)

> Marlo was **more excited** than her brother. (greater)

> This street is **less clean** than the one where I live. (lesser)

The greater form of the comparative degree is formed by adding "er" to the positive degree or by inserting "more" before the positive form.

> rich + er = **richer**

> rich + more = **more rich**

The lesser form of the comparative degree is formed by inserting "less" before the positive form.

> rich + less = **less rich**

Note: Use the comparative degree when comparing only two things.

The **superlative degree** indicates that the quality described by an adjective exists in the **greatest or least degree** in one person or thing.

> Rufus is the **friendliest** dog I know. (greatest)

> Florence seems the **least nervous** of us all. (least)

Note: Use the superlative degree when comparing more than two things.

10i   Some adjectives do not follow the regular methods of forming their comparative and superlative degrees.

Positive degree	Comparative degree	Superlative degree
good	better	best
bad	worse	worst
little	less, lesser	least

(A dictionary will provide the irregular comparisons of such adjectives.)

Most adjectives of three syllables or more are compared by the use of "more" and "most," rather than by the endings "er" and "est."

> Tim is **more capable** of managing a business than Jon.

> Alma is the **most wonderful** girl I know.

10j   Avoid double comparisons which are formed by adding both "more" or "most" and "er" or "est."

Alan is the **brightest** little boy.
(**Not:** ...the **most brightest**. . . .)

Eric is a **better** eater than his brother.
(**Not:** ...a **more better** eater. . . .)

10k   **When two things are compared, both things should be clearly accounted for.**

These clothes look cleaner than **those** (clothes).

George looks older than **he** used to.

An ellipsis is the leaving out of one or more words that are grammatically important but that are understood by the reader.

Harvey plays soccer better than **I** (do).

While (he was) waiting for the pitch, Al Bumbry clenched the bat tightly.

Incomplete subordinate clauses that cause confusion, similar to the confusion caused by **dangling modifiers**, may be corrected by supplying the missing words.

Margaret's dress was torn while **she was** climbing over the fence.
(**Not:** Margaret's dress was torn while climbing over the fence.)

Use the word "other' or "else" to separate the thing being compared from the rest of the group of which the word is a part.

This car gets better mileage than all the **other** cars.

Mary Beth is more beautiful than anyone **else** around.

10l   **Infinitives, infinitive phrases, participles, and participial phrases may act as adjectives.**

Mr. Garcia is the man **to know** if you want a bank loan. (infinitive as adjective)

This is a day **to remember always.** (infinitive phrase as adjective)

Screaming, Nancy woke up from her nightmare. (present participle as adjective)

Covering his face, the defendant walked past the reporters. (participial phrase as adjective)

10m **Infinitive and participial phrases that begin a sentence must be able to refer, both logically and grammatically, to the subject of the main clause.**

> **To qualify for the job, you** need a high school diploma.
> (**Not:** To qualify for the job, a high school diploma is needed. A "high school diploma" cannot apply for the job.)

> **Rushing to finish, Tina** made some errors.
> (**Not:** Rushing to finish, some errors were made by Tina. "Errors" cannot rush to finish.)

10n **Infinitive and participial phrases are called dangling modifiers if they cannot logically and grammatically attach to the subject of the main clause.**

> **To apply for a credit card,** an application form must be filled out. (infinitive phrase as dangling modifier)

> **Being an only child,** my parents spoiled me. (participial phrase as dangling modifier)

Sentences with dangling modifiers may be corrected either by supplying the subject that the phrase can sensibly modify or by changing the phrase to an introductory adverbial clause.

> To apply for a credit card, **one** must fill out an application. (Or: **When one applies for a credit card,** an application form must be filled out.)

> Being an only child, **I** was spoiled by my parents. (Or. **Because I am an only child,** I was spoiled by my parents.)

10o **A prepositional phrase may act as an adjective**

> The violent storm damaged the roof **of our house.**

> Her leaving **without saying a word** irritated me.
> (also considered a **gerund phrase**)

10p **A subordinate clause may act as an adjective**

> Thanks for the present **that you gave me.**

> The woman **who can help you** is not at her desk.

> This ring, **which belonged to my grandmother,** is valuable.

> The building **where they used to live** is being torn down.

> There is never a time **when Ed isn't busy.**

Subordinate clauses that act as adjectives may state essential information or nonessential information.

> The train **that you need to take** is leaving from Track 12. (information essential to describe which train)

> Peter loves his car, **which he hasn't finished paying for.** (information this is nonessential to describe which car)

10q Restrictive and nonrestrictive clauses

Restrictive clauses, which contain essential information, are not set apart by commas.

> The secondhand radio **that I bought for five dollars** works beautifully. (restrictive clause)

Nonrestrictive clauses, which contain secondary information that is not essential to the sentence, are set off by commas.

> My friend Dina, **whom I've known for years,** wants me to visit her. (nonrestrictive clause)

10r "Whose" is the possessive form for the relative pronouns "who," "which," and "that."

> The boy **whose** father died had to get a job.

> The dog **whose** leg was broken runs well now.

> Mr. Temple, **whose** wife is a ballerina, teaches French.

> The book **whose** cover is damaged is half price.

10s A word, phrase, or clause should be placed as close as possible to the word it modifies.

> Give me a glass of **cold** beer.
> (**Not:** Give me a cold glass. . . .)

> We need someone **with experience** to cook breakfast.
> (**Not:** We need someone to cook breakfast with experience.)

> Grant wore a felt hat **that was obviously too small on his head.**
> (**Not:** Grant wore a felt hat on his head that was obviously too small.)

10t **A misplaced modifier is a word, phrase, or clause that is misplaced in the sentence so that it modifies the wrong word.**

Wrong: Mrs. Kent was injured while preparing her husband's dinner in a horrible manner.

Right: Mrs. Kent was injured in a horrible manner while preparing her husband's dinner.

Wrong: The old farmer went to the barn to milk the cow with a cane.

Right: The old farmer with the cane went to the barn to milk the cow.

Wrong: The flames were extinguished before any damage was done by the Fire Department.

Right: The flames were extinguished by the Fire Department before any damage was done.

10u **Squinting modifiers** are modifiers that are misplaced so that the reader cannot tell if the word, phrase, or clause modifies the words immediately before the modifier or immediately after.

Wrong: Henry said **today** he would wash his car.

Right: **Today** Henry said he would wash his car. (Or: Henry said he would wash his car **today.**)

Wrong: The dentist told him **frequently** to use dental floss.

Right: The dentist **frequently** told him to use dental floss. (**Or:** The dentist told him to use dental floss **frequently.**)

CHAPTER 11

Modifiers (continued) – Adverbs, Adverbial Phrases and Clauses

11a **Adverbs modify verbs, adjectives, and adverbs.**

> Don runs **slowly.** (modifies verb)
>
> Emily is an **extremely** gifted pianist. (modifies adjective)
>
> Eric Heiden skates **incredibly** well. (modifies adverb)

11b **The five kinds of adverbs are classified by the questions they answer.**

How? Adverbs of manner.

> She sings **well.** He speaks **clearly.**

Where? Adverbs of place or direction.

> Take me **home.** She was just **here.** He went **out.**

When? Adverbs of time.

> Bring it **immediately.** I'll see you **tomorrow.**

How much? Adverbs of degree or measure.

> That's **enough.** A little **more,** please.

Why? Adverbs of cause, reason, or purpose.

> He left **because** he was afraid.
>
> I have ten dollars, **so** we can go out.

11c **The following words can be either adjectives or adverbs, depending on their use.**

above	fast	only
better	first	slow
cheap	hard	well
deep	long	
early	much	

> The sign said to drive **slow.** (adverb)
>
> **Slow** drivers can be dangerous. (adjective)
>
> Mark Spitz can swim **better** than I can. (adverb)
>
> Lucy feels **better** now. (adjective)

11d Distinguish carefully **when an adverb should follow a linking verb** and **when a predicate adjective should be used** to follow the linking verb.

> Sharon looks **bad.** (predicate adjective meaning that Sharon doesn't look healthy)
>
> Miguel looks **badly.** (adverb meaning that Miguel is doing a poor job looking for something)
>
> Carmen smells **sweet.** (predicate adjective meaning that Carmen has a sweet scent)
>
> Roses smell **sweetly.** (adverb **incorrectly** meaning that roses sniff the air sweetly!)

11e While speaking, one may incorrectly drop the "ly" ending from common adverbs.

> I'm **real** glad you called.
>   (**Correct:** I'm **really** glad you called.)
>
> He **sure** is lucky.
>   (**Correct:** He **surely** is lucky.)

Do not drop the "ly" ending unless a shorter form is correct.

> I bought it **cheaply.** (Or: I bought it **cheap.**)
>
> Come **quickly!** (Or: Come **quick!**)

The adverbs "hardly," "scarcely," "only," and "barely" should not be used with a negative verb construction

> Ernie has hardly any free time.
>   (**Not:** Ernie **hasn't** hardly any free time.)
>
> Rose and I have scarcely worked this week.
>   (**Not:** Rose and I **haven't** scarcely worked this week.)

11f **An adverb may show greater or lesser degrees** of its characteristic quality

> Peter arrived **early.**
>
> Adam came **earlier** than Peter.
>
> Amy came **earliest** of all.

The positive degree simply names the quality expressed by an adverb.

> Stephanie runs **quickly.**

The **comparative degree** indicates that the quality described by an adverb exists for one person or thing to **a greater or lesser degree** than for another person or thing.

> New air conditioners run **more efficiently** than old ones.

> Nat draws **less well** than Monica.

The **comparative degree** of adverbs is formed by inserting **"more" or "less" before the positive degree form**, unless there is an irregular form for the comparative degree.

> Charles works **more diligently** than Mark.

> Barbara gets angry **less often** than Steven.

> This stereo sounds **better** than mine. (irregular form)

The **superlative degree** indicates the quality described by the adverb exists in the **greatest or least degree** for one person or thing.

> Ben works **most carefully** when someone is watching.

> Elaine explained the problem the **most clearly**.

> His was the **least carefully** written report.

The **superlative degree** of adverbs is formed by inserting **"most" or "least" before the positive degree form**.

> Who was voted **"most likely"** to suceed"?

> Tracy Austin played **least skillfully** during the first set.

When two persons or things are being compared, the comparison should be clear.

> I love chocolate more than **Umberto** does.
> (**Not:** I love chocolate more than Umberto. Such an incomplete comparison might be interpreted to mean that I love chocolate more than I love Umberto.)

11g An infinitive or an infinitive phrase may be used as an adverb.

> Robert was willing **to go.** (infinitive used as adverb)

> I am writing **to explain my behavior last night.** (infinitive phrase used as adverb)

11h A prepositional phrase may be used as an adverb.

> We left **for the weekend.**

> The old man sat **on the park bench.**

> The coach supported his team **in every way.**

11i A subordinate clause may be used as an adverb.

Mrs. Maurillo forgot her umbrella **when she left.**

Because they cooperated with him, the president thanked several members of Congress.

11j **An adverb or an adverbial phrase should be placed as close as possible to the word it modifies.**

Joanne worked **without complaining** while her husband went to school.
(**Not:** Joanne worked while her husband went to school **without complaining.**)

Note how an adverbial misplacement may change the meaning of a sentence.

The room can be painted **only** by me.
(not by anyone else)

The room can **only** be painted by me.
(not wallpapered)

Only the room can be painted by me.
(not the outside of the house)

11k **An adverbial clause may be placed either at the beginning of a sentence or, in its natural order, after the main clause.**

After you have read this letter, you will understand my reasons.

You will understand my reasons **after you have read this letter.**

Note: An adverbial clause is followed by a comma when it is used to introduce a sentence.

11l **Adverbial phrases and clauses should be placed so that only one meaning is possible.**

After the movie we all agreed to go for some ice cream. (Or: We all agreed to go for some ice cream **after the movie.**
(**Not:** We all agreed **after the movie** to go for some ice cream.)

Ask Kay to call me **when she gets in.** (Or: **When she gets in,** ask Kay to call me).
(**Not:** Ask Kay **when she gets in** to call me.)

CHAPTER 12
Connectives

12a   A connective joins one part of a sentence to another part.

Phillip **and** Dennis are giving a concert tonight.
(The connective "and" joins the two parts of the compound subject.)

Did you go out **or** did you stay home last night?
(The connective "or"' joins the two independent clauses.)

The banks are closed **because** today is a holiday.
(The connective "because" joins the main clause to the subordinate clause.)

The investigation **of** the robbery has been completed.
(The connective "of" joins the noun "robbery" to the noun "investigation.")

12b   A connective may be a preposition, a conjunction, an adverb, or a pronoun.

Josie left her scarf **on** the bus. (preposition)

Mr. Fernandez campaigned for the presidency **but** he lost. (conjunction)

Kevin looked back **because** someone was shouting. (conjunction)

Ernie left his home an hour ago; **therefore**, he should be here any minute. (adverb)

The letter **that** was mailed this morning should arrive tomorrow. (pronoun)

12c   Prepositions as connectives

A preposition may be **a word or a compound.** A compound consists of two or more words that function as one word.

Come **over** here. (word)

Women live longer than men **according to** statistics. (compound)

12d   A preposition joins a noun or pronoun to the rest of the sentence.

One   prep.↓   of   the **windows** is broken. (noun)

Josh is worried prep.↓ about his **health.** (noun)

These bags have nothing prep.↓ in   **them.** (pronoun)

Choosing the correct preposition is often based on idiomatic usage
— that is, the way English is used, whether or not it contradicts
strict grammatical rules.

12e Some commonly used prepositional idioms are the following:

absolve	from	[blame]
abstain	from	[drinking]
accede	to	[a request]
accommodate	to	[a situation]
accompanied	by	[a lady (**a person**)]
accompanied	with	[applause (**a thing**)]
account	for	[one's actions]
account	to	[one's superior]
acquit	of	[a crime]
adapted	to	[his requirements]
adapted	from	[a novel]
adept	in	[selling a product]
adequate	to	[the demand]
adequate	for	[her needs]
agree	to	[a proposal (**an idea**)]
agree	with	[the teacher (**a person**)]
amenable	to	[an offer]
angry	with	[my cousin (**a person**)]
angry	at	[a remark (**a thing**)]
annoyed	by	[the noise (**a thing**)]
annoyed	with	[the child (**a person**)]
appreciative	of	[their efforts]
averse	to	[hard work (**an idea**)]
basis	for	[agreement]
capable	of	[getting high marks]
concur	with	[the mayor (**a person**)]
concur	in	[the decision (**an idea**)]
confer	with	[someone (**a person**)]
confer	about	[something (**a thing**)]
conform	to	[the rules]
correspond	to	[what I said (**a thing**)]
correspond	with	[his lawyer (**a person**)]
differs	from	[her sister (**a person**)]
differs	with	[what was done (**a thing**)]

disappointed	in	[you (**a person**)]
disappointed	with	[the result (**a thing**)]
enter	into	[an agreement]
enter	upon	[a career]
excepted	from	[further responsibility]
exempt	from	[taxes]
expect	from	[your investment (**a thing**)]
expect	of	[his assistant (**a person**)]
familiar	to	[me (**a person**)]
familiar	with	[the proceedings (**a thing**)]
free	of	[his wife (**a person**)]
free	from	[her nagging (**a thing**)]
identical	with	[something else]
ignorant	of	[his rights]
incompatible	with	[fellow workers]
independent	of	[his relative]
infer	from	[a statement]
involved	in	[a project (**a thing**)]
involved	with	[a friend (**a person**)]
liable	to	[damages (**a thing**)]
necessity	for	[food (**a thing**)]
necessity	of	[avoiding trouble (**doing something**)]
proficient	in	[a skill]
profit	by	[knowledge]
responsible	to	[the owner (**a person**)]
responsible	for	[paying a debt (**a thing**)]
talk	to	[the group (**one person talks**)]
talk	with	[my friends (**all talk**)]
variance	with	[another]
wait	at	[the church (**a place**)]
wait	for	[your uncle (**a person**)]
worthy	of	[consideration]

12f   Prepositions should not be used needlessly.

Where is your brother?
(**Not:** Where is your brother **at?**)

Where are you going?
(**Not:** Where are you going **to?**)

Pete started on another project.
   (**Not:** Pete started **in** on another project.)

We agreed to divide the housework.
   (**Not:** We agreed to divide **up** the housework.)

Prepositions are sometimes left out by mistake.

Irene talked to me **about** her new job and **about** why she left her old one.
   (**Not:** Irene talked to me about her new job and why. . . .)

Dr. Rosen was puzzled **by** and concerned **about** Ellen's nightmares.
   (**Not:** Dr. Rosen was puzzled and concerned about. . . .)

Note: Two different prepositions are needed for this last sentence.

12g   Conjunctions as connectives

A conjunction is a word that joins words, phrases, clauses, or sentences.

Nixon **and** Agnew ended their political careers by resigning (words joined)

The mouse ran out of the kitchen **and** into the living room. (phrases joined)

Casino gambling in Atlantic City has helped some **but** it has hurt others. (clauses joined)

Sally has the ability to do the job; **however,** she has too many personal problems. (sentences joined)

12h   Conjunctions are coordinate, correlative, or subordinate.

A **coordinate conjunction** and a **correlative conjunction** connect grammatical elements of equal rank. A **subordinate conjunction** connects grammatical elements of unequal rank.

12i   Coordinate conjunctions include the following words in order to connect two equal elements.

and, but, or, nor, so, yet

On our vacation we will go to Boston **or** to Cape Cod. (two phrases)

My two favorite colors are blue **and** green. (two words)

I told Stanley that I couldn't leave my house, **so** he should come over tonight. (two subordinate clauses)

Phil was eager to try the new restaurant, **but** he moved away before trying it. (two independent clauses)

12j Correlative conjunctions include the following **word pairs** in order to connect two equal elements.

> either . . . or, neither . . . nor, not only . . . but also,
> both . . . and, if . . . then, since . . . therefore

Take **either** the dark meat **or** the light meat. (two words)

Not only has Rick quit school, **but** he has **also** left town. (two independent clauses)

Both the Baltimore Orioles **and** the Pittsburgh Pirates won the pennant in 1979. (two words)

I have seen her **neither** in the movies **nor** on television. (two phrases)

Note: The correlative conjunctions "neither... nor" should never be written "neither... or.")

Each member of the pair of correlative conjunctions must be followed by the same grammatical construction.

same construction
Woody Allen is **not only** a good **comedian, but also** a good film **director.**

(**Not:** Woody Allen **not only**   is   a good comedian, but **also**
different construction
a good film director.)

same construction
Either we should spend the night here **or** we should leave right now.

different construction
(**Not: Either** we should spend the night here **or** leave right now.)

12k Conjunctive adverbs

A **conjunctive adverb** may be considered a **type of coordinate conjunction.**

Conjunctive adverbs include the following words which **serve to connect two equal elements.**

> therefore, however, consequently, accordingly,
>
> furthermore, besides moreover, nevertheless, still

Although the clause introduced by a conjunctive adverb is grammatically independent, it is logically dependent on the preceding clause for complete meaning.

A storm knocked down our electric wires; **therefore,** we had to eat by candlelight.

A bad traffic accident ahead of us caused us to be delayed; **nevertheless,** we made the party on time.

You have not paid your rent for six months; **accordingly,** I am going to see a lawyer.

Independent clauses joined by a conjunctive adverb should be separated by a semicolon (;) or a period.

Frank and Marty delayed their vacation one week; **consequently,** I was able to join them.

The judge awarded custody of the child to its mother. **Moreover,** the judge set strict guidelines for visiting privileges.

Certain phrases may act as conjunctive adverbs.

Eunice wanted to buy a fur coat; **on the other hand,** she was trying to save money for a car.

We saw many interesting towns and cities on our tour. **In addition,** we met several nice people.

12l Join only the **same parts of speech** with coordinate conjunctions or with correlative conjunctions. **Faulty parallelism will result if different parts of speech are combined.**

Correct: Jim's day consisted of waking up early, working all day, **and** going back to bed. (three gerund phrases)

Faulty: Jim's day consisted of waking up early, working all day, **and** then to go back to bed. (two gerund phrases combined with an infinitive phrase)

Correct: The president's plan was a disappointment **not only** to the leaders of big business, **but also** to the leaders of organized labor. (two prepositional phrases)

Faulty: The president's plan was a disappointment **not only** to the leaders of big business, but also the leaders of organized labor. (one prepositional phrase and one noun)

12m   Connecting elements of unequal rank

A less important idea should be put into a subordinate clause; the more important idea should be expressed in the main or independent clause.

main idea   subordinate idea

Bill is going to work for his father, although he was offered other jobs.

12n   **Subordination may be introduced by a subordinate conjunction, by a relative pronoun, or by a relative adverb.**

Eva will want to go straight to bed **after** she comes back from her exercise class. (subordinate conjunction)

I bought the sneakers **that** you wanted. (relative pronoun)

We saw the house **where** they filmed "Gone with the Wind." (relative adverb)

A subordinate conjunction introduces an adverbial clause.

My mother can knit a sweater **while** she watches television. (adverbial clause tells **when**)

Tell me what he looks like **so that** I'll recognize him. (adverbial clause tells **why**)

12o   **Some relative pronouns introduce adjective clauses.**

Everyone wants a job **that** he likes.

The woman **who** walked across the United States has written a book about her experience.

Bobby gave Connie a new tennis racket, **which** she needed.

Other relative pronouns introduce noun clauses.

Tell me **what** you did.

This book has **whatever** you want to know about scuba diving.

Invite **whomever** you like.

12p   **A relative adverb introduces an adjective clause.**

Do you remember the night **when** we locked ourselves out of the house?

Chris will be at the place **where** we met him last time.

CHAPTER 13

Correct Usage: Choosing the Right Word

"The difference between the right word and the almost-right word is the difference between lightning and the lightning bug (firefly)."

— Mark Twain

13 **A, an.** The indefinite article *a* is used before a consonant sound; the indefinite article *an* is used before a vowel sound. Say *a plan, an idea.*

Accept, except. *Accept* means *to receive; except* when used ·as a verb means *to leave out.* (We *accepted* the gift. Pedro's name was *excepted* from the honor roll.) The word *except* is used most often as a preposition. *Everyone went except me.*

Affect, effect. *Affect* is a verb which means to *influence.* (Winning the sweepstakes will *affect* his attitude.) *Effect,* as a noun, means *an influence.* (Smoking has an *effect* on one's health.) *Effect,* as a verb means to *bring about.* (The teacher's praise *effected* a change in the student.)

Affected, as an adjective, has the meaning of *false.* (She had an *affected* way of speaking.)

Aggravate, irritate. *Aggravate* means to make worse. (Drinking iced water will *aggravate* your cold.) *Irritate* means to *annoy* or *exasperate.* (Mary's continuous chattering *irritated* me.)

Ain't. Do not use this expression.

Already, all ready. *Already* means *before* or *by a certain time.* (Mike said that he had *already* done the job.) *All ready* means *completely ready.* (When the buzzer sounded, the horses were *all ready* to start running.)

All right, alright. The only correct spelling is *all right.*

Altogether, all together. *Altogether* means *entirely, wholly.* (Jane is *altogether* too conceited to get along with people.) *All together* means *as a group.* (After the explosion, the boss was relieved to find his workers *all together* in front of the building.)

Among, between. *Among* is used with more than two persons or things. (The manager distributed the gifts *among* all of the employees.) *Between* is used only with two persons or things. (The steak was divided *between* the two children.)

Amount, number. *Amount* is used to refer to things in bulk. (The war costs a great *amount* of money.) *Number* is used to refer to things that can be counted. (A large *number* of pupils attend this school.)

And etc. This is incorrect. The abbreviation *etc.* stands for the Latin *et cetera.* The *et* means ·and; the *cetera* means *other things.* It is wrong to say *and etc.* because the idea of *and* is already included in the *etc.*

Anyways, anywheres, everywheres, somewheres. These expressions are not correct. Omit the final *s* after each.

As, like. *As,* used as a conjunction, is followed by a verb. (Please do it *as* I told you to.) *Like* may not be used as a conjunction. If it is used as a preposition, it is not followed by a verb. (This ice cream looks *like* custard.)

Awful. See **Terrific, terrible.**

Being that. *Being that* is incorrect for *since* or *because.* (*Since* you are tired, you ought to rest.)

Beside, besides. *Beside* means *alongside of; besides* means *in addition to.* (Nixon sat *beside* Autry at the baseball game.) (There is nobody *besides* her husband who understands Ann.)

Between. See **Among.**

Bring, take. Consider the speaker as a starting point. *Bring* is used for something carried in the direction of the speaker. (When you return from lunch, please *bring* me a ham sandwich.) *Take* is used for something carried away from the speaker. (If you are going downtown, please *take* this letter to the post office.)

Bunch. *Bunch* means cluster. Do not use *bunch* for group or crowd. (This is a large *bunch* of grapes.) (A *crowd* of people were at the scene of the accident.)

But that, but what. Do not use these expressions in place of *that* in structures like the following: I do not question *that* (not *but that*) you are richer than I am.

Can't hardly. Don't use this double negative. Say *can hardly.*

Continual, continuous. *Continual* means happening at intervals. (Salesmen are *continually* walking into this office.) *Continuous* means going on without interruption. (Without a moment of dry weather, it rained *continuously* for forty days and forty nights.)

Could of. Do not use for *could have.*

Data. Although *data* is the plural of *datum,* idiom permits the use of this word as a singular. Some authorities still insist on *Data are gathered* rather than *Data is gathered* or *these data* rather than *this data.* Most persons in computer programming now say *Data is gathered* or *this data.*

Deal. Do not use this term for *arrangement* or *transaction.* (He has an *excellent arrangement* (not *deal*) *with the manager.*)

Different from, different than. *Different from* is correct. *Different than* is incorrect. (His method of doing this is *different from* mine.)

Discover, invent. *Discover* means to see or learn something that has not been previously known. (They say the Vikings, not Columbus, *discovered* America.) *Invent* means to create for the first time. (William S. Burroughs *invented* the adding machine.)

Disinterested, uninterested. *Disinterested* means without bias. (An umpire must be *disinterested* to judge fairly in a baseball game.) *Uninter-*

ested means not caring about a situation. (I am totally *uninterested* in your plan.)

Doesn't, don't. *Doesn't* means *does not; don't* means *do not.* Do not say *He don't* (*do not*) when you mean *He doesn't* (*does not*).

Due to. At the beginning of a sentence, *due to* is always incorrect. Use, instead, *on account of, because of,* or a similar expression. (*On account of* bad weather, the contest was postponed.) As a predicate adjective construction, *due to* is correct. His weakness was *due to* his hunger.

Each other, one another. *Each other* is used for two persons. (The executive and his secretary antagonize *each other.*) *One another* is used for more than two persons. (The members of the large family love *one another.*)

Effect. See **Affect.**

Enthuse. Do not use this word. Say *enthusiastic.* (The art critic was *enthusiastic* about the painting.)

Equally as good. This expression is incorrect. Say, instead, *just as good.* (This car is *just as good* as that.)

Farther, further. *Farther* is used for a distance that is measurable. (The farmer's house is about 100 yards *farther* down the road.) *Further* is used to express the extension of an idea. (A *further* explanation may be necessary.)

Fewer, less. *Fewer* applies to what may be counted. (Greenwich Village has *fewer* conservatives than liberals.) *Less* refers to degree or amount. (*Less* rain fell this month than the month before.)

Flout, flaunt. *Flout* means to mock or insult. (The king *flouted* the wise man when the latter offered advice.) *Flaunt* means to make a pretentious display of. (The upstart *flaunted* his diamond ring.)

Further. See **Farther.**

Get. *Get* means *to obtain* or *receive.* Get should not be used in the sense of *to excite, to interest,* or *to understand.* Say: His guitar playing *fascinates* (not *gets*) me. Say: When you talk about lifestyles, I just don't *understand* (not *get*) *you.*

Good, well. Do not use the adjective *good* in place of the adverb *well* in structures like the following: John works *well* (not *good*) in the kitchen. Jim Palmer pitched *well* (not *good*) in last night's game.

Graduate. One *graduates from,* or *is graduated from,* a school. One does *not graduate a school.* (The student *graduated* [or was graduated] from high school.)

Had of. Avoid this for *had.* Say: My father always said that he wished he *had* (not *had of*) gone to college.

Hanged, hung. When a person is *executed,* he is *hanged.* When anything is *suspended* in space, it is *hung.*

Hardly. See **Can't hardly.**

Healthful, healthy. *Healthful* applies to *conditions that promote health. Healthy* applies to *a state of health.* Say: Stevenson found the climate of Saranac Lake very *healthful.* Say: Mary is a very *healthy* girl.

If, whether. Use *whether* — not *if* — in structures that follow verbs like *ask, doubt, know, learn, say.* Say: Hank Aaron didn't know *whether* (not *if*) he was going to break Babe Ruth's homerun record.

Imply, infer. The speaker *implies* when he suggests or hints at. (The owner of the store *implied* that the patron stole a box of toothpicks.) The listener *infers* when he draws a conclusion from facts or evidence. (From what you say, I *infer* that I am about to be discharged.)

In, into. *In* is used to express a location, without the involvement of motion. (The sugar is *in* the cupboard.) *Into* is used to express motion from one place to another. (The housekeeper put the sugar *into* the cupboard.)

In regards to. This is incorrect. Say *in regard to* or *with regard to.*

Invent. See **Discover.**

Irregardless. Do not use *irregardless.* It is incorrect for *regardless.* (You will not be able to go out tonight regardless of the fact that you have done all of your homework.)

Its, it's. *Its* is the possessive of *it; it's* is the contraction for *it is.*

Kind of, sort of. Do not use these expressions as adverbs. Say: Ali was *quite* (not *kind of* or *sort of*) witty in his post-fight interview.

Kind of a, sort of a. Omit the *a.* Say: What *kind of* (not *kind of a* or *sort of a*) game is lacrosse?

Lay, lie. See "Principal Parts of Irregular Verbs" — page 139.

Learn, teach. *Learn* means *gaining knowledge. Teach* means *imparting knowledge.* Say: He *taught* (not *learned*) his brother how to swim.

Leave, let. The word *leave* means *to depart.* (I *leave* today for San Francisco.) The word *let* means to allow. (*Let* me take your place.)

Less, fewer. See **Fewer, less.**

Liable, likely. *Liable* means exposed to something unpleasant. (If you speed, you are *liable* to get a summons.) *Likely* means probable, with reference to either a pleasant or unpleasant happening. (It is *likely* to snow tomorrow.)

Locate. Do not use *locate* to mean *settle* or *move to.* Say: We will *move to* (not *locate in*) Florida next year.

Might of, must of. Omit the *of.*

Myself, himself, yourself. These pronouns are to be used as intensives. (The Chairman *himself* will open the meeting.) Do not use these pronouns when *me, him,* or *you* will serve. Say: We shall be happy if Joe and *you* (not *yourself*) join us for lunch at the Plaza.

Nice. See **Terrific, terrible.**

Number, amount. See **Amount, number.**

Of, have. Do not use *of* for *have* in structures like *could have.*

Off of. Omit the *of*. Say: The book fell *off* (not *off of*) the shelf.

Pour, spill. When one *pours*, he does it deliberately. (He carefully *poured* the wine into her glass.) When one *spills*, he does it accidentally. (I carelessly *spilled* some wine on her dress.)

Practical, practicable. *Practical* means *fitted for actual work*. *Practicable* means *feasible* or *possible*. Say: My business partner is a *practical man*. Say: The boss did not consider the plan *practicable* for this coming year.

Principal, principle. *Principal* applies to a *chief* or the *chief part* of something. *Principle* applies to a *basic law*. Say: Mr. Jones is the *principal* of the school. Professor White was the *principal* speaker. Honesty is a good *principle* to follow.

Raise, rise. See "Principal Parts of Irregular Verbs" — page 139.

Reason is because. Do not use the expression *reason is because* — it is always incorrect. Say the *reason is that*. (The *reason* Jack failed the course *is that* he didn't study.)

Regardless. See **Irregardless.**

Respectfully, respectively. *Respectfully* means *with respect* as in the complimentary close of a letter, *respectfully yours*. *Respectively* means that each item will be considered *in the order given*. Say: This paper is *respectfully* submitted. Say: The hero, the heroine, and the villain will be played by Albert, Joan, and Harry *respectively*.

Rise, raise. See "Principal Parts of Irregular Verbs" — page 139.

Said. Avoid the legalistic use of *said* like *said letter, said plan, said program* except in legal writing.

Should of. Do not use for *should have*.

Sit, set. See "Principal Parts of Irregular Verbs" — page 139.

Some. Do not use *some* when you mean *somewhat*. Say: I'm confused *somewhat* (not *some*).

Spill, pour. See **Pour, spill.**

Suspicion. Do not use *suspicion* as a verb when you mean *suspect*.

Take, bring. See **Bring, take.**

Teach, learn. See **Learn, teach.**

Terrific, terrible. Avoid "lazy words." Many people don't want to take the trouble to use the exact word. They will use words like *terrific, swell, great, beautiful*, etc. to describe anything and everything that is favorable. And they will use words like *terrible, awful, lousy, miserable*, etc. for whatever is unfavorable. Use the exact word. Say: We had a *delicious* (not terrific) meal. Say: We had a *boring* (not *terrible*) *weekend*.

This kind, these kind. *This kind* is correct — as is *that kind, these kinds*, and *those kinds*. (My little brother likes *this kind* of pears.) *These kind* and *those kind* are incorrect.

Try and.   Do not say *try and*. Say *try to*. (*Try to* visit me while I am in Florida.)

Uninterested. See **Disinterested.**

Wait for, wait on.   *Wait for* means *to await; wait on* means *to serve*. Say: I am waiting *for* (not *on*) Carter to call me on the telephone.

Way, ways.   Do not use *ways* for *way*. Say: It is a long *way* (not *ways*) to Japan.

Where.   Do not use *where* in place of *that* in expressions like the following: I see in the newspaper *that* (not *where*) a nuclear reactor may be built a mile away from our house.

Would of.   Do not use for *would have*.

GRAMMAR AND USAGE INDEX

---

*This Index does not include items listed in Chapter 13 (Correct Usage: Choosing the Right Word). Since these Correct Usage items are in alphabetical order, it will be easy for you to locate any Correct Usage explanation whatsoever.